T0219979

Accelerating Development Velocity Using Docker

Docker Across Microservices

Kinnary Jangla

Apress®

Accelerating Development Velocity Using Docker: Docker Across Microservices

Kinnary Jangla
San Francisco, CA, USA

ISBN-13 (pbk): 978-1-4842-3935-3   ISBN-13 (electronic): 978-1-4842-3936-0
https://doi.org/10.1007/978-1-4842-3936-0

Library of Congress Control Number: 2018962734

Managing Director, Apress Media LLC: Welmoed Spahr
Acquisitions Editor: Louise Corrigan
Development Editor: James Markham
Coordinating Editor: Nancy Chen

Cover designed by eStudioCalamar

Cover image designed by Samuel Zeller on Unsplash

Distributed to the book trade worldwide by Springer Science+Business Media New York, 233 Spring Street, 6th Floor, New York, NY 10013. Phone 1-800-SPRINGER, fax (201) 348-4505, e-mail orders-ny@springer-sbm.com, or visit www.springeronline.com. Apress Media, LLC is a California LLC and the sole member (owner) is Springer Science+Business Media Finance Inc (SSBM Finance Inc). SSBM Finance Inc is a **Delaware** corporation.

For information on translations, please e-mail rights@apress.com, or visit www.apress.com/rights-permissions.

Apress titles may be purchased in bulk for academic, corporate, or promotional use. eBook versions and licenses are also available for most titles. For more information, reference our Print and eBook Bulk Sales web page at www.apress.com/bulk-sales.

Any source code or other supplementary material referenced by the author in this book is available to readers on GitHub via the book's product page, located at www.apress.com/9781484239353. For more detailed information, please visit www.apress.com/source-code.

Printed on acid-free paper

To all those engineers who struggle with ramp-up curves on new software tools!

Table of Contents

About the Author

Kinnary Jangla has worked in the tech industry for a dozen years and is currently an engineering manager at Pinterest in the Ads division. Previously she worked on the machine learning Homefeed infrastructure team where she used Docker to develop the debugging framework.

Kinnary previously worked at Uber and Microsoft, is the author of three books, and holds six patents. You can follow her on Twitter at @kjangla.

About the Technical Reviewer

Michael Irwin is an application architect at Virginia Tech who is striving to modernize how software is developed and run on campus, by driving the adoption of Docker-based workloads, CI/CD pipelines, the public cloud, single-page applications, and more. As a Docker Captain and Community Leader (Meetup Organizer), he has the opportunity to share his expertise and experiences with others but also learn how others are using the latest technologies. When developing, he writes code in Node, Java (Java EE mostly), and JavaScript but actively contributes to projects written in other languages and frameworks. He's blessed to have a beautiful wife and four daughters.

Acknowledgments

Writing a book requires teamwork. I'm lucky to have found a team of thorough tech reviewers such as Michael Erwin and James Markham, who revised my content thoroughly to ensure that this book is completely most up to date. Thanks, Apress, for the opportunity, and Nancy Chen, for all the hard work of coordination and keeping me on schedule.

This book took a long time to complete. In the past few months, I wanted to give up multiple times. It was my husband's push and support that ultimately got me to the finish line. I can never thank you enough, Abhinav Vora.

Thank you to all my family and friends for being so patient and understanding of the lack of time and attention I was able to devote to you these past months. Your support and motivation kept me going.

Introduction

The idea of writing this book occurred to me while I was ramping up on Docker during my first year at Pinterest. There is a lot of content on the Internet, but it is unstructured and sometimes incorrect and inaccurate. This book will help you to understand the fundamentals of Docker. To understand anything in depth, it's best to start with basic concepts. Over the past years, the needs of tech companies have evolved significantly. This book will help you understand the need for Docker in the software industry and how Docker has managed to ease the growing pains of this industry.

I have tried to structure this book by explaining the fundamentals before going into anything specific to Docker. I hope that helps you understand the fundamentals of Docker.

My hope, too, is that this book is useful to both students and engineers who want to ramp up on Docker quickly.

The following sections provide a snapshot of the book.

Chapter 1: Containers

This chapter focuses on what Docker is all about. It's about containers. But what are containers and how do they differ from virtual machines? Why does Docker make use of container technology and what are the benefits of that? What are the advantages and challenges of containerization? At the end of this chapter, you will have learned the underlying technology of Docker.

Chapter 2: Docker

This chapter focuses on how the software industry evolved and what gave rise to the need for containers and, therefore, Docker. In this chapter, you'll learn the history of Docker, in addition to some of its basic use cases today.

Chapter 3: Monolith vs. Microservices

Because this book focuses on debugging microservices using Docker, this chapter talks about the evolution of microservices, the differences between monolith and microservices, and the advantages and challenges of both. It will help you understand why debugging becomes significantly difficult when you're dealing with multiple services that all need to talk to one another.

Chapter 4: Docker Basics

This chapter is all about taking the first few steps to begin working with Docker. This section discusses the terminology used in the Docker world, the underlying architecture of Docker, how to install Docker, and some basic Docker commands. This chapter is your go-to to step foot into Docker land.

Chapter 5: Docker Images

This chapter goes deep into what Docker images are and how they're created. It examines Dockerfiles, which is where all the instructions to build Docker images are located. Then it goes into how to build Docker images and, finally, into Docker containers in depth. I would encourage you to take some extra time to understand the role of Dockerfiles, Docker images, and Docker containers. I'd also advise acquiring a thorough understanding of this chapter.

Chapter 6: Docker Compose

This chapter is devoted to the Docker Compose tool. This links all the services and helps in running an application from end to end. Here you'll learn all aspects of Docker Compose: how to install it, how to use it, and what happens behind the scenes.

Chapter 7: Debugging Microservices Using Docker

This is what the book has been leading to. This chapter is the core and longest chapter of this book. It explains what distributed environments are and their challenges. It later goes into depth about how to debug an end-to-end real-world use case, by explaining different related debugging techniques.

Chapter 8: Advanced Docker Use Cases

After exploring how to debug an application, based on the microservices architecture, this chapter discusses some advanced use cases of Docker. It talks about the use of Docker in a production environment, orchestration using Docker, and offers some tips and tricks to help you with the software.

CHAPTER 1

Containers

A container is any receptacle or enclosure for holding a product used in storage, packaging, and shipping.

Wikipedia, "Container,"
https://en.wikipedia.org/wiki/Container, 2018.

In this chapter, you will learn the basics of containers and how they are used in the software industry. You will also see how containers differ from virtual machines and discover some of the pros and cons of using containers. This chapter puts you on the path to learning about Docker in depth.

What and Why?

You can't work in a software company today and not hear about software containers: Docker, Kubernetes, Mesos, and a host of others. But before we dive into any of this, let's look at what really changed in the world that led to the need for containers.

When you run a program on your machine in a certain environment, and the environment that supports your program on a production machine is not identical, problems arise. You test using a certain version of the programming language, and it runs a different version in production, so something weird happens, owing to the lack of forward

© Kinnary Jangla 2018
K. Jangla, *Accelerating Development Velocity Using Docker*,
https://doi.org/10.1007/978-1-4842-3936-0_1

or backward compatibility. Alternatively, you rely on a certain version of an SSL library, and a different version is installed in production. The network topology or the security policies might be different. These inconsistencies can cause all sorts of problems. Let's take a step back. What is a container in the traditional sense of the word, and how can containers solve this problem?

"A container is any receptacle or enclosure for holding a product used in storage, packaging, and shipping," right? Now let's apply this to software.

The concept of container technology uses this same paradigm of shipping containers in transportation. The idea is that before shipping containers were invented, manufacturers had to be prepared to ship goods in a wide variety of modes—ships, trains, or trucks—with different sized containers and packaging. By standardizing the shipping container, goods could be seamlessly transferred among shipping methods, without any additional preparation. Before the advent of this standard, shipping anything in bulk was a complicated, laborious process.

The promise behind software containers is essentially the same. Instead of shipping via a full operating system (OS) and your software (and maybe the software that your software depends on), you simply pack your code and its dependencies into an image that can then run anywhere, and because these are usually pretty small, you can pack lots of containers onto a single computer.

Put simply, a container consists of an entire runtime environment: an application, plus all the dependencies, libraries and other binaries, and configuration files needed to run it, bundled into one package. By containerizing the application platform and its dependencies, differences in OS distributions and underlying infrastructure are abstracted away.

By allowing software code to be prepped in ready-made software containers, the code can quickly be moved around to run on servers running the Linux OS or be connected to run a distributed app in the cloud. This approach also has the benefit of speeding up the testing process and building large, scalable cloud applications. While this approach has been around in software development circles for many years, it has recently become more popular with the growth of Linux and cloud computing. Earlier projects taking the container approach have included BSD Jails, Solaris Zones, and Unix V7.

Containers vs. Virtual Machines

Heard the terms *virtualization* or *virtual machine*? First, what are virtual machines (VMs)? In the present day and age, when collaborating and working remotely have become commonplace, virtualization is key. Historically, as server processing power and capacity increased, bare metal applications weren't able to exploit the new abundance in resources. Thus, VMs were born, designed by running software on top of physical servers, to emulate a particular hardware system.

At the heart of it, a VM is an app! Typically called hypervisor, it emulates an OS. Hypervisor is a program that enables you to host several different VMs on a single hardware. Everything in the VM is self-contained, and it typically has all the capabilities of the OS it is imitating.

Sounds like a fake computer, doesn't it? However, there are some important distinctions. A VM is indeed entirely virtual, in that it doesn't have any hardware of its own, except for the storage drive it comes from. More modern and complex VMs are supported by server setups.

Virtualization services are usually provided by specific companies, such as VMware, for example.

How do containers compare to VMs, though? Are they the same thing? When do you use what? And what is the key difference, really?

3

VMs take up a lot of system resources. Each VM runs not just a full copy of an OS but a virtual copy of all the hardware that the OS requires to run. This quickly adds up to a lot of RAM and CPU cycles. In contrast, all that a container requires is enough of an OS, supporting programs and libraries, and system resources to run a specific program.

What this means in practice is that you can put many more applications on a single server with containers than you can with a VM.

OS virtualization has grown in popularity over the last decade, to enable software to run predictably and well when moved from one server environment to another. But containers provide a way to run these isolated systems on a single server or host OS.

Containers sit on top of a physical server and its host OS, for example, Linux or Windows. Each container shares the host OS kernel. Binaries and libraries are the only elements created from scratch. Containers are thus exceptionally "light"—they are only megabytes in size and take just seconds to start, as opposed to gigabytes and minutes for a VM.

Containers also reduce management overhead. Because they share a common OS, only a single OS requires care and feeding for bug fixes, patches, and so on. This concept is similar to what we experience with hypervisor hosts: fewer management points but slightly higher fault domain. In short, containers are lighter weight and more portable than VMs.

VMs and containers differ in several ways, but the primary difference is that containers are isolated processes running on an OS that are implemented using namespaces. With VMs, the hardware is virtualized to run multiple OS instances. Containers' speed, agility, and portability make them yet another tool to help streamline software development.

Figure 1-1 provides a comparison of containers and VMs.

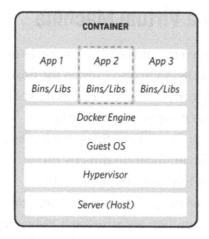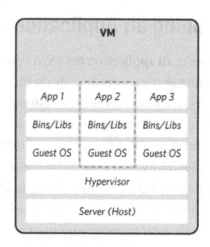

Figure 1-1. *Containers vs. virtual machines*

Pros and Cons of Containerizing Applications

Let us start with understanding how applications are run traditionally. That will help us understand what containerization is not.

Running an Application on a Host Machine

Traditionally, you would install an application on a host computer and run it directly from a host computer's file system. The environment this application runs in would include the host's file system, network interfaces, ports, devices, etc. To get the application working, you would additionally require other packages that your application depends upon. You might also want different versions of the same package running on your system.

Besides this, running multiple instances of your service on the host computer might get tricky, because the application might bind to a particular network port by default; other services might bind to the same network port; the service might have to read configuration files on service startup; etc.

5

Running an Application on a Virtual Machine

Running an application on a VM can overcome some of the drawbacks of running applications directly on the host OS. A VM also runs on the host, but it has its own kernel, file system, network interfaces, etc. This makes it easy to keep almost everything inside the OS separate from the host.

Because a VM is a separate entity, you don't have the same issues of inflexibility that arise from running an application directly on hardware. You could run an application ten times on the host by starting up ten different VMs. The service on each VM could listen on the same port number and not cause a conflict, because each VM could have a different IP address, as if it's a different computer altogether, except that it's not.

Likewise, if you have to shut down a host computer, you could either migrate the VM to another host (if your virtualization environment supports it) or just shut it down and start it again on the new host.

The downside of running each instance of an application in a VM is the resources it consumes. Your application might require only a few megabytes of disk space to run, but the entire VM could consume many gigabytes of space. Also, the startup time and CPU consumption of the VM is almost sure to be higher than the application itself would consume.

Containers offer an alternative to running applications directly on the host or in the VM, which can make the applications faster, more portable, and more scalable.

Advantages of Using Containers

Containers offer both efficiency of resources and flexibility of usage. While VMs take up several gigabytes of space, containers are sized within the range of tens to hundreds of megabytes. A server can host significantly more containers than VMs because of the lack of the need to run multiple copies of OSs. Flexibility comes from the container being able to carry all the files it needs with it. As with an application running in a VM, it can have its own configuration files and dependent libraries, as well as its own network interfaces that are distinct from those configured on the host. So, a containerized application is easier to move around than its directly installed counterparts, and it doesn't have to contend for such resources as port numbers, because each container they run in has separate network interfaces.

Because the container can hold the application and its dependencies it requires to run, the startup time, disk space consumption, and processing power is much lower than those of a VM. Containers also don't have a separate kernel, as does a VM. Using containers can decrease the time required for development, testing, and deployment of applications and services. Testing and bug tracking also become less complicated, because there is no difference between running your application on a test server vs. production.

Containers are a very cost-effective solution and can potentially help you decrease your operating and development costs. Container-based virtualization is a great option for microservices, developer operations, and continuous deployment.

Challenges of Using Containers

One of the main disadvantages of container-based virtualization compared to traditional VMs is security. Containers share the kernel and other components of the host OS. This means that containers are less isolated from each other than VMs, which have their own OS. If there is a vulnerability in the kernel, it can jeopardize the security of all containers. VMs only share the hypervisor, which makes them less prone to attacks than the shared kernels of containers.

While VMs with any kind of OS can reside next to each other on the same server, you must start a new server, to be able to run containers with different OSs. For complex enterprise applications, this can be a serious constraint.

In addition to that, deploying containers in a sufficiently isolated way while maintaining an adequate network connection can be tricky too. Also, containers, as they are designed, cannot see other containers by default. So, what happens when you want your container to work closely with another container? For example, what if your service requires access to a database server?

Some of these problems are addressed by Docker, which you will read about in the next chapter.

Summary

This chapter described the basics of containers, their use in the software industry, and how they differ from VMs. It also described the difference between running an application on a host machine vs. a VM vs. a container. It discussed the advantages and challenges of using containers.

This chapter has put you on a path along which you can start from scratch, if you're new to the world of virtualization, by comparing the differences between all options available today and the reasons the software industry has moved toward containerization rather than other available options.

CHAPTER 2

Docker

Docker is another term for longshoreman. Longshoreman: a person employed by a port to load and unload ships.

`https://www.collinsdictionary.com/us/dictionary/english/docker`

In the last chapter, you saw what containers are and the differences between them and virtual machines (VMs). You also read about some of the advantages of containers and the challenges of using them.

Docker provides a solution to some of the problems posed by containers. But why did Docker become so successful only in recent years? Let's look into that a little .

In this chapter, you will learn about the evolution of Docker and the reasons for its wide adoption by the software industry. You will learn some basics of Docker, some basic use cases for it, and some of its main components. We'll dive deeper into this in the future chapters.

History

As new as containerization and Docker might sound to you, the intriguing wrinkle is that they're really not new. The idea of containers has been around since the early days of Unix, with the `chroot` command. Rings a bell? Docker software was originally built on Linux containers, which were introduced in 2008.

As you should know from having read Chapter 1, containerized applications share a common operating system (OS) kernel, eliminating the need for each instance to run its own separate system. An application can be deployed in seconds and uses a lot fewer resources than hypervisor-based virtualization. However, because applications rely heavily on a common OS kernel, this approach can work only for applications that share the exact OS version. Docker found a way to address this limitation.

Docker was released as an open source project by dotCloud, Inc., in 2013. dotCloud is a San Francisco–based technology startup founded by the French-born American developer and entrepreneur Solomon Hykes. It relies heavily on namespaces and cgroups to ensure resource isolation and to package an application along with its dependencies, which are mostly Linux kernel features. It is this clustering of dependencies into a package that lets an application run across different platforms and still support a level of portability. This also allows developers to develop in the language of their choice, on a platform of their choice. This flexibility is what attracted a lot of interest in recent years.

Docker became extremely famous in many fast-growing companies that were trying to build test and dev environments for developers that could replicate production systems in many ways. Today, Docker is used by some well-known companies, including PayPal, Spotify, Yelp, and Pinterest, which are finding value in the software.

Let's look at a time line of Docker milestones, according to the *Container Journal.* Docker source code was released as an open source software in March 2013. Needless to say, everyone had access to it after that. About a year later, Docker built the `libcontainer` framework, which it switched to. Around the same time, demand for orchestration tools increased, as Docker kept getting popular. In order for Docker containers to scale, orchestration frameworks are key. In June 2014, Google introduced Kubernetes, which helped Docker scale. Later that year, Amazon's EC2 container service, which is a cloud-based container as a service, was offered. In June 2015, the open container initiative, which promotes open standards related to containers, was launched.

A year later, Docker acquired a small company working on unikernels technology called Unikernels. By June of 2016, Docker had become very popular with the container ecosystem. It included the Swarm orchestrator in its platform, even though it was replaceable. Later that year, Docker started supporting all versions of Microsoft Windows. By 2016, Docker was extremely successful, and major companies began using it extensively for their most important use cases.

Now that we've reviewed how Docker became a success in the industry, let's dive deeper into what Docker is and what use cases it solves.

What Is Docker?

Docker is the name of the company that produces the software called Docker. It is also the open source project that is now called Moby. When someone refers to *Docker,* he or she can be referring to any of these three things. Let's try to understand a bit about each of them.

Docker is a software that runs on Linux and Windows. It is a tool designed to make it easier to create, deploy, and run applications, by using containers. The software is developed in the open, as part of the Moby open source project on GitHub.

Docker is a tool that is mainly designed for developers, so that they can focus on developing on their choice of platform, without having to worry about the OS the application will eventually run on. It allows them to run end-to-end workflow without having to get into services they don't understand. In other words, it helps them to obtain a clearer view of the entire stack fairly easily. Additionally, running Docker containers has no additional memory overhead, so multiple Docker containers running multiple services creates very low overhead.

Understanding the different parts of Docker will help us get a good overview of everything Docker is made of before we dive deeper into any of it. The Docker architecture is explained in detail in Chapter 4.

The Docker Runtime and Orchestration Engine

The Docker engine is the infrastructure plumbing software that runs and orchestrates containers. This means that all the Docker, Inc., and third-party products plug into the Docker Engine and build around it. It is combined with a workflow for building and managing your application stacks. It is this underlying client-server technology that builds and runs containers using Docker's components and services. It is made up of the Docker daemon, a server that is a type of long-running program; a REST API, which specifies interfaces that programs can use to talk to the daemon and tell it what to do; and the CLI, the command-line interface that talks to the Docker daemon through the API. Many docker applications use the underlying API and CLI.

In other words, the Docker Engine is the program that creates and runs the Docker container from the Docker image file. So, next, let's take a quick look at what a Docker image file is.

Docker Images

A Docker image is not just a file; it is more of a file system. This file system is composed of multiple layers, and each layer contains a file of the contents for that layer that cannot be changed. In other words, it is *immutable*. It is essentially a snapshot of a Docker container.

Docker images are created with the build command. They produce a container and are stored in a Docker registry. Images can become fairly large quite quickly. Therefore, they are designed to be composed of layers of other images, allowing a minimal amount of data to be sent when transferring images over a network.

To explain this more clearly with a programming metaphor, if an image is a class, then a container is an instance of a class—a runtime object. Containers are lightweight and portable encapsulations of an environment in which you can run applications.

An image is created using a Dockerfile. Let's see what a Dockerfile is. Later on, we'll learn how to build a Docker image from a Dockerfile in detail, in Chapter 5. For now, let's take a quick look at what Dockerfiles are all about.

Dockerfiles

Everything starts with a Dockerfile. It is a text document that contains a set of instructions or commands to assemble an image that are understood by the build engine.

The Dockerfile defines what goes in the environment inside your container. Access to resources, mapping volumes, passing arguments, copying files that must be inside your container, etc., go into this file. After creating the Dockerfile, you will have to build it to create the image of the container. The image is just the snapshot of all the executed instructions in the Dockerfile. Once you have this application image built, you can expect it to run across any machine using the same kernel.

Why Should You Use Docker?

Docker provides application isolation with little overhead. By saving space with the low memory footprint, it has some powerful advantages.

Primarily, you can benefit from the extra layer of abstraction (in which code and its dependencies are packed together) offered by Docker. Another significant advantage is that you can have many more containers running on a single machine than you can with virtualization alone, owing to Docker's lightweight nature.

Another significant advantage is that containers can be spun and shut down within seconds. The Docker FAQ has a good overview of what Docker adds to traditional containers.

Let's look at some of the key uses.

Docker's Key Use Cases

Here are some of the key use cases that Docker supports that promote consistency of environments.

Configuration Management

Simplifying configurations is one of the primary use cases of Docker. One of the features it provides is the ability to run any application or platform with its own config on any OS or other infrastructure. Docker provides the capability of clubbing your environment with your configuration into code, packaging it, and deploying it.

Code Pipeline Management

When you have simplified your application configuration, code management becomes a lot simpler as a result. Code lives in many different environments before it reaches a point at which it can be shipped. It first lives in the developer's machine, where it is tested, then it goes to test environments, where it might be deployed on test machines. Only after that does it reach the production servers.

All these environments vary in infrastructure, settings, configuration, etc. With Docker, a consistent environment is provided across these different phases, which in turn ease the development and deployment process. The ease with which Docker images can be spun helps you to maintain consistency across runtime environments.

Developer Productivity

As mentioned earlier, the life cycle of shipping an application goes through numerous phases, starting from the developer machine all the way to the production servers. At all points, we mostly strive to ensure a consistency between test and production environments.

To achieve this, every service must reflect how it will run in the production environment. For that to be possible, test environments require all the dependent services that end up taking huge amounts of space.

Docker comes in handy here by allowing a bigger number of services to run simultaneously, by not adding to the memory footprint. Docker's shared code volumes make it available to the container's host OS, which helps to support low memory usage.

This works amazingly well for developers, because they can use the code editor of their choice on a platform of their choice to develop the application, without worrying about the OS the application will run in on a production setting. This also helps developers avoid getting into the nitty gritty of services they don't really understand but still enables them to test their end-to-end scenarios, which implicitly helps them understand the full stack better.

Faster Deployment

Prior to the existence of VMs, spinning up new hardware was a very cumbersome and time-consuming process. With VMs, that process became slightly easier, and with Docker, it became exponentially easier.

Creating and destroying Docker containers, bringing up a new container, etc., become extremely simple with Docker, not to mention less costly, which in turn allows for better resource allocation.

Application Isolation

When multiple microservices power up an application, it is very likely that these services depend on common libraries and packages, but possibly different versions of them. If you were to start an application on a single machine, getting all these services up and running to kick-start the application would practically be impossible, owing to the version conflicts of the various dependencies.

For that reason, isolating these microservices in their own environments, with only their dependencies and configurations that don't conflict with other services, lets that service run independently. Setting up all these microservices in their independent Docker containers and having these containers communicate with each other seems like an ideal solution to getting an application up and running seamlessly.

Continuous Integration and Continuous Deployment

Docker has the ability to do image versioning. This means that you can set up your Docker containers to pull new code from your code repository, build it, package it in a Docker image, and push this new image to your image repository. Your deployment tool can then pull the newest image from your image repository, deploy it to your test environments, and, finally, promote it to your production environments. You could do this either every time there is new code in your repository or at a certain frequency, depending on how often you require your code to be deployed.

Consistent Environments Across Machines

How often have you observed that something works on your coworkers' machines but not on yours? Docker helps you prevent this situation completely, by setting consistent environment variables and configuration settings in the image file, so that your and your coworkers' machines look the same, without any other variables that can affect the run of an application or service.

Summary

In this chapter, you learned how Docker evolved, how it went from being an open source project in 2013 to acquiring unikernels to running natively on Windows. You saw what requirements of the software industry gave rise to the wide adoption of Docker. You also learned some basics of Docker and its components. We'll dive deeper into this in future chapters.

Finally, you learned some of the key use cases of Docker, ranging from code pipeline management to faster deployments to increasing developer productivity. These are just some of the use cases of Docker that are widely applied across the software industry.

In the next chapter, you will learn about the differences between monoliths and microservices and when and why you use one vs. the other. You will see how to use Docker with microservices, as well.

CHAPTER 3

Monolith vs. Microservices

A monolith is "a large single upright block of stone, especially one shaped into or serving as a pillar or monument."

Oxford Living Dictionaries, s.v. "monolith,"
`https://en.oxforddictionaries.com/definition/monolith`,
accessed October 1, 2018.

Docker provides a solution to some of the problems posed by containers. But why did Docker become so successful only in recent years? Let's delve into that a bit.

In the previous chapter, you learned about the evolution of Docker and the reasons for its wide adoption by the software industry. You also learned some basic use cases of Docker and its components.

In this chapter, I will consider the evolution of the microservices architecture. You'll see how challenges posed by a monolith system, such as difficulty in continuous deployments, testing, scalability, etc., were solved by adopting a microservices architecture. You will also learn about the challenges of a microservices architecture and how application isolation enabled by Docker can come to the rescue.

© Kinnary Jangla 2018
K. Jangla, *Accelerating Development Velocity Using Docker*,
https://doi.org/10.1007/978-1-4842-3936-0_3

Before we get into microservices, however, let's first understand how microservices and service-oriented architectures are related. Both are architectures based on distributed systems, but there are some fundamental differences.

Microservices architecture is a kind of service-oriented architecture. In both architectures, services have a certain responsibility. These services can be developed independently on different tech stacks, and in both architectures, developers must deal with the complexity of a distributed system. However, microservices architecture splits an application into multiple different services that can be independently developed, scaled, tested, and deployed, whereas in a service-oriented architecture, services are provided to other application components. A service-oriented architecture must be deployed as a monolith, and all services must follow the same communication protocol.

Now let's look at how microservices evolved.

Evolution of Microservices

Before we go into learning how microservices evolved, let's first look into challenges presented by monoliths, because that is what contributed to the need for microservices architecture.

A monolith application is a single, self-contained software application in which all components of the application, including the user interface and the data access code, are all tightly coupled into a single program.

While a monolith service is simple to implement, test, deploy, and perhaps even scale, there are many other challenges that can arise as the complexity of the software application increases. Here are some of the challenges:

- It becomes more and more difficult to test different pieces of the application independently.

- Continuously deploying the entire application becomes tedious.

- If you change a piece of code in a certain area, you will have to deploy the entire service, which could seem quite long and unnecessary.

- A software bug in any module can bring the entire service down. Monoliths have single points of failure, which are very difficult to debug.

- As the size of a monolith application increases, the startup time of the application keeps increasing with it.

- To adapt new frameworks and technologies in your monolith app that uses a single stack, you must rewrite the entire application.

To mitigate all of these potential pitfalls, microservices architecture was born.

A microservices architecture is one in which a monolith is split into multiple smaller services that operate independently of each other but are interconnected. Each microservice is an independent service or an independent application. Different microservices in an application can be built on different software stacks and implement their own architecture. What's more, in a microservices architecture, each microservice can additionally implement its own database schema, as required, instead of sharing a single database schema. It can also use a database that best suits its need. As a matter of fact, microservices should use their own databases and database schema; otherwise, the dependency on shared databases and schemas doesn't really allow the services to be independent. Figure 3-1 shows two services using MySQL but different instances of it. The monolith is broken down into multiple services, each of which uses its own database.

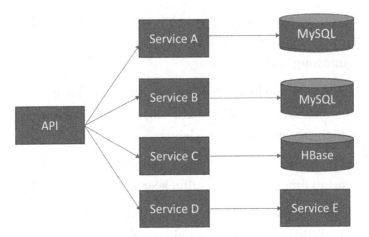

Figure 3-1. *Microservices architecture in which an application is broken down into multiple services, and each service uses its own independent database*

Microservices have many advantages over monoliths. A microservice architecture deals with the complexity issue of a monolith, for which it helps in dividing a single application into multiple components. This makes understanding as well as maintaining the code base a lot easier. Because the services operate independently, they can be developed using a framework that best suits the need. This gives developers a lot of flexibility, as they are free to choose what works best. Different modules can be deployed independently of one another. Services can also be scaled, as required. Testing independent services becomes easier as well, owing to the modularity that comes with a microservices architecture.

Comparing Monoliths and Microservices

Table 3-1 provides a consolidated view of a monolith vs. a microservices architecture.

Table 3-1. *Differences Between Monolith and Microservices*

	Monolith	**Microservices Architecture**
1. Maintenance	Maintenance grows in complexity as the application does.	It is easier to maintain microservices, as they are modular and independent.
2. Deployment	Continuous deployment becomes very difficult as the monolith keeps growing.	Deployment of individual services is easier, and services can be deployed as and when required.
3. Testing	Testing the entire monolith becomes a pain.	Testing individual components is much easier.
4. Startup time	As the monolith grows in size, the startup time increases with it.	Startup times of individual services are much faster, because they are smaller in size.
5. Adoption of newer technologies	A monolith is written in a single language, uses a single database, and is averse to adopting newer technologies.	Developers are free to choose the technologies to build their microservices. Each microservice can also use a database that best suits its needs. Microservices architecture allows you to take advantage of the latest available technologies.
6. Scalability	It's much harder to scale a complex monolith.	Microservices can be scaled on demand, as and when needed.

Challenges with Microservices

While microservices address many issues with monoliths, they introduce many other kinds of problems that present a challenge. With a microservices architecture, you are dealing with all challenges that come with a distributed system. For example, because services in a microservices architecture are interconnected, inter-service communication must occur, and for that, a single, reliable, and consistent communication channel must be established, for example, using HTTP.

Multiple services mean more management of those services. All of these must be independently managed for their health and maintenance. These services have to be frequently updated and upgraded to meet the newest versions of the dependencies they use.

Microservices might have their own logging mechanisms. This might result in lots of unstructured and potentially unmanaged data. Retrieving logs can become confusing with gigabytes of available logging data.

Finding the root cause of a failure in a certain workflow might be very tedious to debug. In order to debug an entire workflow, you might have to get multiple services up and running and then test them end to end, in order to know where the bug exists, because the logic is distributed, as is the data. There could also be cyclic dependencies between services, which can be very difficult to deal with while debugging the root cause of a failure.

Last, the most significant issues are those related to versioning. When more than one service depends on certain libraries or packages, but only different versions of those libraries, it becomes tricky to get these services up and running. How can you have two versions of the same dependency on your machine? If you can't have that, how can you manage getting these services up and running, either in a production system or in your debugging environment?

For example, imagine a spellchecker application with three different microservices: service A, service B, and service C. When the user enters a word to check the spelling of, the request is sent to service A, which depends on JavaScript version 1.8.5, Python version 2.7, and Flask version 0.12.4. Service B takes the request from service A, checks the spelling against a dictionary, and sends it to service C. In order to get service B up and running, you need Flask version 0.10.3. Service C takes this spelling and writes it to a database for records. Service C depends on Python version 2.1.

Table 3-2 shows the dependencies required on your machine, to get these services up and running successfully.

Table 3-2. Service dependencies

Service A	Service B	Service C
JavaScript v1.8.5	-	-
Python v2.7	-	Python v2.1
Flask v0.12.4	Flask v0.10.3	-

As you see, getting service A and service B running on the same machine is practically impossible, because they both require a different version of Flask. Similarly, getting service A and service C running successfully on a single machine is also impossible, owing to the different versions of Python.

This is one of the most prevalent and widely seen problems in the software industry. A common solution might be to update your services to use the same version of a certain dependency. But in a complex application with thousands of microservices, this becomes extremely difficult to keep track of. So, what is a good solution here? Docker.

In the preceding example, if you isolate service A, service B, and service C in their own environment and let them run independently and, at the same time, enable inter-process communication between them, they would not conflict with one another. Docker enables exactly this!

In the next few chapters, I will delve into how exactly this problem can be solved with the help of Docker, in addition to the many other advantages of using Docker to solve related problems.

Summary

In this chapter, you saw how the microservices architecture was born and how it evolved. The many challenges that came with monolith services were solved by the microservices architecture.

You also saw the differences between a monolith and a microservices architecture. You saw how as an application grows in size and complexity, a monolith poses many problems, such as difficulties with continuous deployments, testing, scalability, startup, etc. These are elegantly solved by a microservices architecture.

Last, you saw that with a microservices architecture come all the challenges of a distributed system. You saw how getting multiple services up and running can be quite challenging, if they rely on different versions of the same dependencies. Application isolation comes in very handy here. And Docker can help us with that.

In the next chapter, I will get into the basics of Docker and explain the nitty-gritties, including related terminologies, its architecture, how to install Docker, and some basic commands to use to get started.

CHAPTER 4

Docker Basics

Essential foundations, starting points, and fundamentals

In this chapter, we will look into the Docker terminology that has been used in the previous chapters of this book and which I will continue to use in future chapters.

You'll see the different components of the Docker architecture, including the Docker Engine, Docker Hub, Docker clients, Docker host, and Docker registries. You'll see how different Docker objects are created by the Docker daemon and how Docker Hub can be used to pull existing Docker images and buy, sell, or distribute images for free.

Additionally, you will learn how to install Docker on the Mac operating system (OS) platform.

I will examine more closely some of the basic Docker commands, providing an example of the use of each command, so that you can play around with it and then follow it with your own example.

© Kinnary Jangla 2018
K. Jangla, *Accelerating Development Velocity Using Docker*,
https://doi.org/10.1007/978-1-4842-3936-0_4

Terminology

Before you begin to approach the fundamentals of Docker, it is important to learn the associated lingo. Following are certain keywords and phrases that you will come across frequently, now that you're on the path to becoming a Docker expert!

> *Image*: A Docker image is a bundle of all the dependencies and configurations that an application depends on to run successfully. An image is this package that runs inside a container. Once an image is created, it cannot be changed. In other words, a Docker image is immutable.

> *Container*: A Docker container is a lightweight instance of a Docker image. It is a running process that has been isolated using namespaces and uses the image for its root file system.

> *Dockerfile*: A Dockerfile is a text file that contains instructions to build a Docker image.

> *Building a Dockerfile*: This refers to building the instructions in the Dockerfile, in order to create a Docker image that can then run inside a Docker container.

> *Compose*: This refers to a command-line tool that operates on one or more files that are a composition of multiple Dockerfiles of different applications/ services, in a sense. With the Compose tool, you can run a single YAML file and get the images build to create and have them all running together.

Architecture

Before mastering Docker, let's get into how it all works behind the scenes, to get a solid understanding of how it really works and how its different components interact with one another.

To begin with, let's look at Docker's different components:

- Docker platform

- Docker Engine

- Docker architecture

  - Docker client

  - Docker daemon

  - Docker registries

- Docker objects

  - Images

  - Containers

  - Services

- Docker Hub

As you have seen in the previous chapters, some of the advantages of Docker are process- and application-level isolation, portability, and ease of deployment and testing. Many different components come into play to support these scenarios. So, let's delve into the components one at a time.

Docker Platform

Docker provides a platform to bundle dependencies and other information, such as environment variables, configurations, settings, etc., into a single isolated environment. Owing to this isolation, dependencies across applications do not interfere with each other, and, hence, multiple applications can run inside their own containers. These containers can all run simultaneously on a single host machine. Because containers are different than virtual machines (VMs), in that they don't need a hypervisor later and can run directly on the host machine's kernel, a lot more containers can run on a single hardware machine than if you were to use VMs.

The Docker platform also provides the ability to manage your containers, allowing you to develop and test your applications using containers. When ready, you can also deploy your application in its production environment, using containers.

Docker Engine

The Docker Engine is a client-server application. It consists of the following three parts, as shown in Figure 4-1.

1. A server process, also known as a daemon process. This is a background process that is continuously running and constantly listening to the REST API interface for any commands to process.

2. A REST API interface that programs can talk to, in order to communicate with the Docker daemon. This can be accessed by an HTTP client.

3. A client that is a command-line interface (CLI).

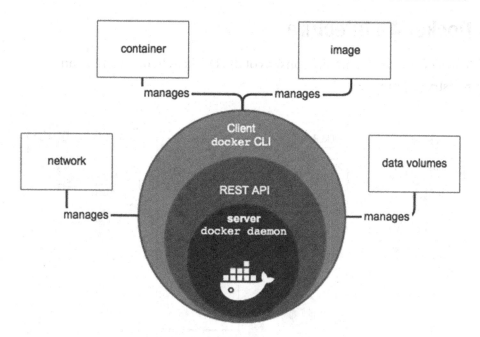

Figure 4-1. *Docker Engine architecture*

The way to get anything done using Docker is through the Docker client, via the CLI or a script composed of commands. The client then communicates these commands, via the REST API, to the Docker daemon, which is the server. The Docker daemon then gets the job done. It creates such Docker objects as images, containers, volumes, etc.

Let's look more extensively into Docker's client-server architecture.

Docker Architecture

The Docker system mainly consists of the Docker client, daemon, and registry (Figure 4-2).

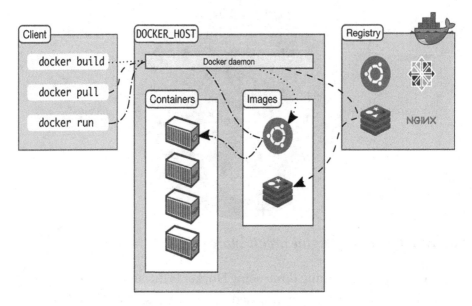

Figure 4-2. *Docker client-server architecture*

Docker Client

The Docker Client is the primary way in which most users interact with Docker. When you run commands using the CLI, these commands are then sent to the Docker daemon, using the Docker API interface. The Docker daemon or the *dockerd* then executes these commands and creates relevant Docker objects. The Docker client has the ability to communicate with multiple Docker daemons.

Docker Daemon

The Docker daemon is a server process that is persistent in nature and runs in the background. It continuously listens to the REST API interface and looks for any incoming requests to process commands. The daemon can listen to the API interface using different socket types, such as Unix, TCP (transmission control protocol), and FD (file descriptor).

Docker Registries

The images created by the Docker daemon must be stored at a certain location, for ease of access. The Docker registry is this location. There are public registries, such as the Docker Hub, that can be used by anyone. By default, Docker looks for images on the Docker Hub, but this can be configured to use your private registry as well.

Commands such as Docker pull retrieve the required images from your configured registry and Docker push pushes the image to this same configured registry.

From a Docker store, you can buy, sell, or distribute images for free. You can then use these images to deploy an application in your test or production environment.

Let's move forward a bit and look at the different objects of Docker that have been referenced multiple times in this book so far.

Docker Objects

With the use of Docker, different objects are generated, mostly by the Docker daemon. Some of these objects are images, containers, services, and storage.

Images

A Docker image is a read-only file system that contains instructions to create a container that can run an application. Most of the time, a Docker image is based on another image and is customized. You could either use existing images published in public registries, such as the Docker Hub, or create your own image.

A Dockerfile is used to build a Docker image. A Dockerfile contains simple instructions that can be understood by the Docker daemon, to create the image and run it.

Docker images are layers that correspond to each instruction in the Dockerfile. A part of what makes a Docker image super lightweight is that when you modify a part of the Dockerfile, only that layer is modified, rather than the entire image.

Containers

A Docker container is an instance of an image. An image runs inside a container. You can manage a container using `stop`, `start`, and `delete` commands. Multiple containers can be connected to one another through a network. They can be connected to storage, and they can also talk to one another.

As you have seen in Chapter 1, containers are much more lightweight than VMs, owing to their startup times being very fast.

In order to create a container, an image, in addition to the container's configuration and settings, is provided. When a container is deleted, everything related to the container is also deleted, including state and storage.

The Docker run command is used to run a container. When you run this command, the following things happen:

1. The Docker image is pulled from the configured registry.

2. A new Docker container is created.

3. A local file system is allocated to that container, to enable creation and modification of files and directories in its local file system.

4. The container is connected to the default network, unless you configure a networking option.
   A container is assigned an IP address.

5. Docker starts running the container and attaches it to your local terminal. This allows you to interact with this container.

6. You can stop or remove the container, using your terminal input, at any time.

Services

In a distributed application, different functionalities of the app constitute different services. For example, if you are building an application for suggestions based on keywords entered by the user, you might want a front-end service that takes the word and sends it to the service that verifies the legitimacy of the word. This might, in turn, go to another service that might execute an algorithm, in order to generate the suggestions, etc., which are then returned to the service.

These are all different services on different Docker containers that sit behind different Docker daemons. These Docker daemons are all connected through the network and interact with each other. To the user, this might look like a single application that runs, but behind the scenes, these are multiple services that make the entire application function.

All these services work together as a swarm, managed by different managers and workers. Each swarm contains a Docker daemon. These daemons communicate with each other using the Docker API.

A Docker Compose YAML file is used to get all these services up and running together. Later, in Chapter 6, you will see how to use the Docker Compose tool in detail.

Docker Hub

Docker Hub is the primary location for storage of Docker images. It is a cloud-based public registry from which you can pull images or push images to. It also links to Docker Cloud. It is a centralized store for image discovery and distribution. By default, Docker is configured to use this public registry.

A user can buy or sell Docker images from the Docker Hub. Alternatively, a user can also distribute Docker images for free on the hub. A user can search for Docker images using the Docker Hub user interface or the CLI.

```
kinnaryjangla@dev-abc: docker search alpine
```

NAME	DESCRIPTION	STARS	OFFICIAL	AUTOMATED
alpine	A minimal Docker image based on Alpine Linux...	4203	[OK]	
mhart/alpine-node	Minimal Node.js built on Alpine Linux	379		[OK]
anapsix/alpine-java	Oracle Java 8 (and 7) with GLIBC 2.28 over A...	346		
gliderlabs/alpine	Image based on Alpine Linux will help you wi...	177		
frolvlad/alpine-glibc	Alpine Docker image with glibc (~12MB)	162		[OK]
alpine/git	A simple git container running in alpine li...	46		[OK]
kiasaki/alpine-postgres	PostgreSQL docker image based on Alpine Linux	42		[OK]
zzrot/alpine-caddy	Caddy Server Docker Container running on Alp...	32		[OK]
easypi/alpine-arm	AlpineLinux for RaspberryPi	30		
davidcaste/alpine-tomcat	Apache Tomcat 7/8 using Oracle Java 7/8 with...	30		[OK]
byrnedo/alpine-curl	Alpine linux with curl installed and set as ...	17		[OK]
etopian/alpine-php-wordpress	Alpine WordPress Nginx PHP-FPM WP-CLI	15		[OK]
hermsi/alpine-sshd	Dockerize your OpenSSH-server upon a lightwe...	12		[OK]
davidcaste/alpine-java-unlimited-jce	Oracle Java 8 (and 7) with GLIBC 2.21 over A...	11		[OK]
hermsi/alpine-fpm-php	Dockerize your FPM PHP 7.2 upon a lightweigh...	10		[OK]
alpine/socat	Run socat command in alpine container	10		[OK]
graze/php-alpine	Smallish php7 alpine image with some common ...	9		[OK]
yobasystems/alpine-xen-orchestra	Xen Orchestra running on Alpine Linux [docke...	8		[OK]
masterroshi/xmrig-alpine	Cryptonote CPU Miner wrapped in a Alpine Doc...	8		[OK]
spotify/alpine	Alpine image with `bash` and `curl`.	5		[OK]
tenstartups/alpine	Alpine linux base docker image with useful p...	5		[OK]
functions/alpine	Alpine Linux / BusyBox with the OpenFaaS wat...	4		
govuk/gemstash-alpine	Gemstash server running on Alpine	3		[OK]
casept/alpine-amd64	A basic alpine linux image.	0		
smartentry/alpine	alpine with smartentry	0		[OK]

Now that we have looked behind the scenes at how Docker actually operates, let's see how to install it.

Installing Docker

There are two Docker editions available to install.

Docker Community Edition (CE): This works for small communities or individual developers looking to get started and experiment with Docker.

Docker Enterprise Edition (EE): This is meant for enterprises that use Docker to ship business-critical applications that need to scale.

For the purposes of this book, let's look at how to install the Docker CE. Docker CE is available for both the Mac and Windows OSs. It is also available to Amazon Web Services and Microsoft Azure.

Let's look at how to install Docker CE on the Mac OS platform. There are some system requirements to meet before you can install Docker on your machine. You will need a Mac machine model that is at least from 2010 or later. In addition, you will need at least 4GB of RAM.

1. Go to the Docker store at `https://store.docker.com/editions/community/docker-ce-desktop-mac` and click Get Docker, from the right-side pane, as seen in Figure 4-3.

Get Docker Community Edition for Mac

Docker for Mac is available for free.

Requires Apple Mac OS Yosemite 10.10.3 or above.
Download Docker Toolbox for previous OS versions.

By downloading this, you agree to the terms of
the Docker Software End User License Agreement

 Get Docker

Figure 4-3. *Getting the Docker Community Edition for Mac*

2. Once you have the dmg file on your machine,
double-click it and drag Moby the whale to the
Applications folder, as shown in Figure 4-4.

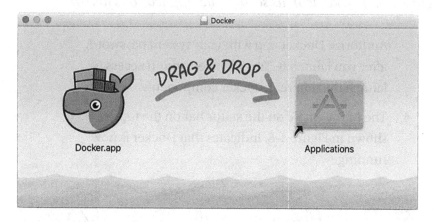

Figure 4-4. *Drag Moby to your Applications folder*

3. In the Applications folder, double-click the Docker
    app, as seen in Figure 4-5.

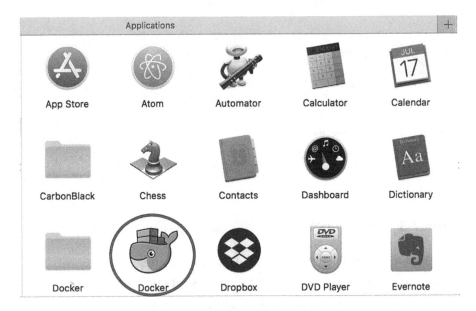

Figure 4-5. *Docker icon as seen in the Applications folder*

> Authorize Docker.app with your system password,
> after you launch it. You will need admin access to
> launch the different Docker components.

4. The Moby whale on the status bar on the top, as
    shown in Figure 4-6, indicates that Docker is now
    running.

Figure 4-6. *Docker icon on the status bar*

5. If you have successfully installed the app, you will
    also see a pop-up with a success message, next
    steps, and tips, as shown in Figure 4-7.

Figure 4-7. *Successful installation of Docker shows a pop-up with next steps*

To dismiss this pop-up, click the whale on the top status bar.

6. Right-clicking the whale on the status bar will give you options to set or modify your preferences, as shown in Figure 4-8.

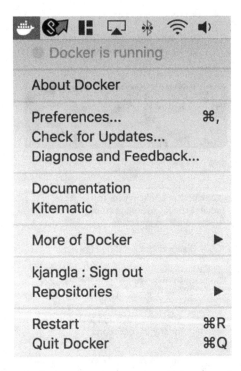

Figure 4-8. *Right-click Docker menu on the status bar icon*

7. Check About Docker, to ensure you have the latest version.

Now that we have Docker installed and running on our machines, let's take a look at some basic Docker commands, so that you can play around and experiment with them.

Basic Docker Commands

Following are some basic Docker commands that you can start playing with.

docker container run

This runs a command in a new container. When a user runs the Docker run command, it isolates the containers in its environment and the configuration within its own local file system.

The Docker run command specifies an image, in order to run that image inside a container.

The basic docker container run command looks like this:

```
docker container run  [OPTIONS]  IMAGE  [COMMAND]  [ARG...]
```

Image is the existing image you want to run inside the container. With docker container run [OPTIONS], the developer can modify the defaults of the images. Some options types are

-d: You can choose to let the container run in the background, in detached mode, or in the foreground. By default, when -d is not specified, the container runs in the foreground.

-a: The foreground mode lets you attach your local console to the process's (running inside the container) standard input output.

docker container create

The docker container create command lets you create a new container from an existing image that has been built previously. This is shown following. The –t command stands for "tty," which sets a pseudo time of the container to live, and the -I command stands for "interactive" and keeps the standard input open, even if it's not attached.

Usage:

```
docker container create  [OPTIONS]  IMAGE [COMMAND]  [ARG...]
```

Example:

```
kinnaryjangla@dev-abc:~/code/test$ docker container create -t
-i myApp bash
38001kjhasd7qhs8whs7sh38729wajsh352191j888dhasg2
kinnaryjangla@dev-abc:~/code/test$
```

docker container start

The docker container start command lets you start a new container or a container that has been previously stopped, as shown here. The –t flag stands for "tty" and is used to give the container a pseudo time to live. The -I flag keeps the standard input open, even when it's not attached.

Usage:

```
docker container start [OPTIONS] CONTAINER [CONTAINER...]
```

Example:

```
kinnaryjangla@dev-abc:~/code/test$ docker container create -t -i
myApp bash 38001kjhasd7qhs8whs7sh38729wajsh352191j888dhasg20
kinnaryjangla@dev-abc:~/code/test$ docker start -a -i 38001kjhasd
root@38001kjhasd:/mnt/myApp #
```

docker container stop

The docker container stop command lets you stop a currently running container.

Usage:

```
docker container stop [OPTIONS] CONTAINER [CONTAINER...]
```

Example:

```
kinnaryjangla@dev-abc:~/code/test$ docker container stop
38001kjhasd
```

docker image build

The docker image build command builds the docker image using the
instructions in the Dockerfile.

Usage:

```
docker image build [OPTIONS] PATH | URL | -
```

Example:

```
kinnaryjangla@dev-abc:~/code/test$ docker image build myApp/.
Sending build context to Docker daemon  1.649MB
Step 1/6 : FROM openjdk:8
 ---> ef09cb43251e
Step 2/6 : ENV CONFIG_FILE config/myApp.dev.properties HEAP_
SIZE 4G LOG4J_CONFIG_FILE config/log4j.dev.properties NEW_SIZE
2G JAVA_COMMAND java
 ---> Using cache
 ---> 09c7e98f7c49
Step 3/6 : WORKDIR /opt/myApp
 ---> Using cache
 ---> 3c29b8fa2f25
Step 4/6 : ARG ARTIFACT_PATH=target/myApp-0.1-SNAPSHOT-bin.tar.gz
 ---> Using cache
 ---> c563d2e7990c
Step 5/6 : ADD $ARTIFACT_PATH /opt/myApp/
Successfully built bd6110589d1b
```

docker image pull

The docker image pull command pulls an image from a docker registry.

Usage:

```
docker image pull [OPTIONS] NAME[:TAG|@DIGEST]
```

Example:

```
kinnaryjangla@dev-abc:~/code/test$ docker image pull alpine
Using default tag: latest
latest: Pulling from library/alpine
8e3ba11ec2a2: Pull complete
Digest: sha256:7043076348bf5040220df6ad703798fd8593a0918d06d3ce
30c6c93be117e430
Status: Downloaded newer image for alpine:latest
kinnaryjangla@dev-abc:~/code/test$
```

docker search

You can search for Docker images using the docker search command.

Usage:

```
docker search  [OPTIONS]  TERM
```

Example:

```
kinnaryjangla@dev-abc::~/code/test$ docker search alpine
```

NAME	DESCRIPTION	STARS	OFFICIAL	AUTOMATED
alpine	A minimal Docker image based on Alpine Lin...	4203	[OK]	
mhart/alpine-node	Minimal Node.js built on Alpine Linux	379		
anapsix/alpine-java	Oracle Java 8 (and 7) with GLIBC 2.28 over...	346		[OK]
gliderlabs/alpine	Image based on Alpine Linux will help you ...	177		[OK]
frolvlad/alpine-glibc	Alpine Docker image with glibc (~12MB)	162		[OK]
alpine/git	A simple git container running in alpine ...	46		[OK]
kiasaki/alpine-postgres	PostgreSQL docker image based on Alpine Linux	42		[OK]
zzrot/alpine-caddy	Caddy Server Docker Container running on A...	32		[OK]
easypi/alpine-arm	AlpineLinux for RaspberryPi	30		
davidcaste/alpine-tomcat	Apache Tomcat 7/8 using Oracle Java 7/8 wi...	30		[OK]
byrnedo/alpine-curl	Alpine linux with curl installed and set a...	17		[OK]
etopian/alpine-php-wordpress	Alpine WordPress Nginx PHP-FPM WP-CLI	15		[OK]
hermsi/alpine-sshd	Dockerize your OpenSSH-server upon a light...	12		[OK]
davidcaste/alpine-java-unlimited-jce	Oracle Java 8 (and 7) with GLIBC 2.21 over...	11		[OK]
hermsi/alpine-fpm-php	Dockerize your FPM PHP 7.2 upon a lightwei...	10		[OK]
alpine/socat	Run socat command in alpine container	10		[OK]
graze/php-alpine	Smallish php7 alpine image with some commo...	9		[OK]
yobasystems/alpine-xen-orchestra	Xen Orchestra running on Alpine Linux [doc...	8		[OK]
masterroshi/xmrig-alpine	Cryptonote CPU Miner wrapped in a Alpine D...	8		[OK]
spotify/alpine	Alpine image with `bash` and `curl`.	5		[OK]
tenstartups/alpine	Alpine linux base docker image with useful...	5		[OK]
functions/alpine	Alpine Linux / BusyBox with the OpenFaaS w...	4		
govuk/gemstash-alpine	Gemstash server running on Alpine	3		[OK]
casept/alpine-amd64	A basic alpine linux image.	0		[OK]
smartentry/alpine	alpine with smartentry	0		

docker image ls

The docker image ls command is used to list all the Docker images on the host machine.

Usage:

```
docker image ls  [OPTIONS]  [REPOSITORY[:TAG]]
```

Example:

```
kinnaryjangla@dev-abc:~/code/test$ docker image ls
```

REPOSITORY	TAG	IMAGE ID	CREATED	SIZE
ubuntu	latest	cd6d8154f1e1	3 days ago	84.1MB
openjdk	7	bd6110589d1b	4 days ago	472MB
alpine	latest	11cd0b38bc3c	2 months ago	4.41MB

docker container ps

The docker container ps command is used to list all containers running on the host.

Usage:

```
docker container ps  [OPTIONS]
```

Example:

```
kinnaryjangla@dev-abc:~/code/test$ docker container ps
```

CONTAINER ID	IMAGE	COMMAND	CREATED
e55ce4b2e4f5	alpine	"./bin/docker_run_..."	6 days ago
119b4b5eed95	ubuntu	"./bin/docker_run_..."	6 days ago

docker container rm

The docker container rm command is used to remove one or more containers. You cannot remove a running container without the -f flag to force it, which first stops the container and then removes it. In order to do that, you must first stop the container, using docker container stop <container-id>. This command execution is shown following:

Usage:

```
docker container rm [OPTIONS] CONTAINER [CONTAINER...]
```

Example:

```
kinnaryjangla@dev-abc:~/code/test$ docker container stop
e55ce4b2e4f5
kinnaryjangla@dev-abc:~/code/test$ docker image rm 119b4b5eed95
```

docker container inspect

This command allows you to inspect the details of a container.

Usage:

```
docker container inspect [OPTIONS] CONTAINER [CONTAINER...]
```

Example:

```
kinnaryjangla@dev-abc:~/code/test$ docker container inspect
f9d4b5c9aa49
[
    {
        "Id": "f9d4b5c9aa49fb22b23ae0d377236e1da80ceebc14c
        67550e36f6c0345eb2062",
        "Created": "2018-08-03T06:11:54.181815872Z",
        "Path": "/test/bin/entry_point.sh",
        "Args": [],
```

```
"State": {
    "Status": "running",
    "Running": true,
    "Paused": false,
    "Restarting": false,
    "OOMKilled": false,
    "Dead": false,
    "Pid": 30163,
    "ExitCode": 0,
    "Error": "",
    "StartedAt": "2018-08-03T06:11:58.414063235Z",
    "FinishedAt": "0001-01-01T00:00:00Z"
},
"Image": "sha256:b657c637b59170b7ea275d0af93fed7b89b
1c286aeacd54380529559l1a89d7a",
"ResolvConfPath": "/var/lib/docker/containers/f9d4b5
c9aa49fb22b23ae0d377236e1da80ceebc14c67550e36f6c0345
eb2062/resolv.conf",
"HostnamePath": "/var/lib/docker/containers/f9d4b5c9aa
49fb22b23ae0d377236e1da80ceebc14c67550e36f6c0345eb2062/
hostname",
"HostsPath": "/var/lib/docker/containers/f9d4b5c9aa49
fb22b23ae0d377236e1da80ceebc14c67550e36f6c0345eb2062/
hosts",
"LogPath": "/var/lib/docker/containers/f9d4b5c9aa49fb22
b23ae0d377236e1da80ceebc14c67550e36f6c0345eb2062/f9d4b5
c9aa49fb22b23ae0d377236e1da80ceebc14c67550e36f6c0345eb
2062-json.log",
"Name": "/webapp_selenium-chrome_1",
"RestartCount": 0,
"Driver": "overlay",
"MountLabel": "",
```

These are some basic commands you can start to explore. Let's go through a little end-to-end Hello World example.

In the following example, we'll pull an existing Hello World image, run it, and view the images and containers.

1. First, pull the hello-world Docker image. This will pull the image from the Docker Hub registry.

```
kinnaryjangla@dev-abc:~/code/test$ docker image pull
hello-world
Using default tag: latest
Latest: Pulling from library/hello-world
9bbdshfg673e39ja: Pull complete
Digest: sha256:
fkjdh7t6dauadubiadadia8dya98777da9fiudfhd9a86fidfbdfi
d8fydisch
Status: Downloaded newer image for hello-world:latest
```

2. Use docker images to view the image that was just pulled, as shown following.

```
kinnaryjangla@dev-abc:~/code/test$ docker image ls
REPOSITORY    TAG      IMAGE ID      CREATED    SIZE
Hello-world   latest   ekjad89sjdfd 2 months ago
1.85kB
```

3. Now run the hello-world image, which will run this image inside a new container, as follows.

```
kinnaryjangla@dev-abc:~/code/test$ docker container run
hello-world
latest: Pulling from library/hello-world
d1725b59e92d: Pull complete
Digest: sha256:0add3ace90ecb4adbf7777e9aacf18357296e799
f81cabc9fde470971e499788
Status: Downloaded newer image for hello-world:latest
```

Hello from Docker!
This message shows that your installation appears to be working correctly.

To generate this message, Docker took the following steps:

1. The Docker client contacted the Docker daemon.
2. The Docker daemon pulled the "hello-world" image from the Docker Hub.
   (amd64)
3. The Docker daemon created a new container from that image which runs the executable that produces the output you are currently reading.
4. The Docker daemon streamed that output to the Docker client, which sent it to your terminal.

To try something more ambitious, you can run an Ubuntu container with:
 $ docker run -it ubuntu bash

Share images, automate workflows, and more with a free Docker ID:
 https://hub.docker.com/

For more examples and ideas, visit:
 https://docs.docker.com/get-started/

This preceding example lets you go through an end-to-end scenario of pulling an existing Docker image, viewing the image, and running the image.

In the next chapter, we'll take a closer look at how to create Docker images using Dockerfiles and run these images inside Docker containers.

Summary

In this chapter, we looked in detail at the Docker terminology that has been commonly used in the previous chapters of this book and that will continue to be used in future chapters.

We also examined the different components of the Docker architecture, including the Docker Engine, Docker Hub, Docker clients, Docker hosts, and Docker registries. We also saw how different Docker objects are created by the Docker daemon. We saw how Docker Hub can be used to pull existing Docker images and buy, sell, or distribute images for free.

Additionally, you saw how to install Docker on the Mac OS platform in detail.

We looked at some basic Docker commands, with sample usage and examples of each command, so that you can explore them further. We then walked through a simple end-to-end example of pulling the existing Hello World image and running it.

In the next chapter, I'll go more into detail on how to build an image from a Dockerfile and run it inside a container.

Summary

CHAPTER 5

Docker Images

A Docker image is an immutable read-only file system that is a snapshot of the entire package of an application, including the dependencies, configuration, and settings.

In this chapter, you'll learn about Dockerfile and its basics. We'll build images using Dockerfiles and then view the running images. We'll then run these images inside a Docker container, and you'll discover how to attach the container to our local terminal input/output.

Docker Images

As mentioned previously, Docker images are read-only and immutable and created with the `docker image build` command. They are stored inside a Docker registry and run inside a container. Images can become quite large very quickly. Therefore, they are designed to be composed of layers of other images, allowing a minimal amount of data to be sent when transferring images over a network. So, you can build your own customized image on top of an existing image. When you modify that image, new layers are added that contain your changes.

As for Docker containers, you'll learn about them in more detail later in this chapter, but to summarize with a programming metaphor, if an image is a class, then a container is an instance of a class, that is, a runtime object. While images are lightweight and portable encapsulations of an environment, containers are the running instances of images.

© Kinnary Jangla 2018
K. Jangla, *Accelerating Development Velocity Using Docker*,
https://doi.org/10.1007/978-1-4842-3936-0_5

Furthermore, a Docker image is created using a Dockerfile. Let's see what a Dockerfile is. Later on, you'll learn how to build a Docker image from a Dockerfile.

Dockerfile

Everything Docker begins with a Dockerfile. The Dockerfile is the instruction set on how to build an image. It the basis on which your entire Docker container is built. It specifies all the configuration settings environment variables, volumes to be mounted, the base image to build on top of, the list of dependencies, etc. All this is then bundled into an image that then runs inside the container.

A Dockerfile must be built to create the Docker image of an application. The image is just the "compiled version" of the source code that lives inside the Dockerfile. The Dockerfile is a text file that contains a set of instructions or commands that are then assembled into an image.

Creating a Sample Dockerfile

Let's create a sample Dockerfile next. To begin, create a file called Dockerfile inside a directory called `docker`.

```
kinnaryjangla@dev-abc:~/code/docker$ vim Dockerfile
```

Build your Dockerfile using the following commands. Replace the `LABEL maintainer email` with your e-mail address.

```
#This is a sample image
FROM ubuntu
LABEL maintainer="email@example.com"

RUN apt-get update
RUN apt-get install -y nginx
CMD ["echo", "Hello World!"]
```

Let's look at the instructions in the preceding Dockerfile.

1. The first line, #This is a sample image, is a comment. You can add other comments to the Dockerfile for readability using the # command.

2. The FROM keyword is used to tell Docker which base image you want to build your customized image on top of. This instruction is mandatory.

3. LABEL is a non-executable instruction used to indicate the author of the Dockerfile.

4. The RUN instruction is used to execute a command on top of an existing image. That in turn creates another layer with the results of the execution of the command on top of the image. For example, if there is a precondition to install PHP before running an application, you can run appropriate commands to install PHP on top of the base image (say, Ubuntu), as shown following.

   ```
   FROM ubuntu
   RUN apt-get update && update apt-get install -y php
   ```

5. The CMD command doesn't execute anything during the build time. It just specifies the intended command for the image. The difference between the CMD and the RUN command is that RUN actually executes the command during build time. If you have multiple CMD instructions in the Dockerfile, only the last one will take effect.

Following are some other commands that can come in handy when creating the Dockerfile:

- ENV: This instruction can be used to set the environment variables in the container as shown following.

```
#Default environment variables requires to run service,
can be overridden by docker run
ENV CONFIG_FILE=config/config.service.test.properties \
        HEAP_SIZE=6G \
        LOG4J_CONFIG_FILE=config/log4j_local.xml \
        NEW_SIZE=4G
```

- COPY: This instruction is used to copy the files and directories from a specified source to a specified destination (in the file system of the container), as follows.

```
COPY conditions.txt /usr/tmp
```

- ADD: The ADD instruction is like the COPY instruction. It has some additional features, such as support for remote URLs. The COPY instruction is more readable, so if you don't need the extra supported features that ADD provides, it's recommended that you use the COPY instruction instead. See the following usage. Tar or zip files will be auto-expanded when you add one to a source destination.

```
ADD http://www.xyz.com/sample.tar.xz /usr/src
```

- WORKDIR: This is used to set the currently active directory for other instructions, such as RUN, CMD, ENTRYPOINT, COPY, and ADD. See the following paragraph for a usage example.

  If you provide a relative path as the WORKDIR, it will be taken as relative to the path of the previous WORKDIR instruction.

```
WORKDIR   /user
WORKDIR   home
```

- USER: This is used to set the UID (or username) to use when running the image or any subsequent commands. See the following usage.

```
USER daemon
```

- VOLUME: This instruction specifies a path in which data should be persisted longer than the life of the container. See the following usage.

```
VOLUME    /data
```

- ENTRYPOINT: This command is the primary command of your Docker image.

  This command is set in such a way that whenever you run the image, the ENTRYPOINT command will be executed every time.

  You can also pass arguments here, but they are optional. You can pass them when you run the image with something such as docker run <image-name>.

  Also, all the elements specified using CMD will be overridden, except the arguments. They will be passed to the command specified in ENTRYPOINT. Following is a sample usage.

```
CMD   "Hello World!"
ENTRYPOINT   echo
```

Save this file, and in the next section, you'll see how to build an image from this Dockerfile.

Building Images with Dockerfile

As you've learned so far, Docker images are immutable, read-only file systems. Images can be based on other existing images that can be pulled from Dockerfile. This makes modifying them a lot easier, because the only thing that changes is the layer that gets modified. This also prevents images from becoming extremely large in size.

In the previous section, we created a Dockerfile called Dockerfile with some basic instructions and saved it in a directory called docker.

Let's continue to build an image from the Dockerfile created in the previous section. From the docker directory, run the command docker image build. The . builds the Dockerfile within the directory.

When you run this command for the first time, you'll see a long list of packages being pulled, because we're building our image on top of the Ubuntu image.

I am going to divide the output in multiple sections, to make it easier to read. You should be able to see this entire output, if your image is built successfully.

As per the Dockerfile, each instruction is built sequentially. In the following sequence, you see first (Step 1/5) some images get pulled successfully from the base Ubuntu image. Step 2/5 assigns the author of the image to the image. In Step 3/5, the apt-get update command runs on top of the base Ubuntu image.

```
kinnaryjangla@dev-abc:~/code/docker$ docker image build .
Sending build context to Docker daemon  2.048kB
Step 1/5 : FROM ubuntu
latest: Pulling from library/ubuntu
124c757242f8: Pull complete
9d866f8bde2a: Pull complete
fa3f2f277e67: Pull complete
398d32b153e8: Pull complete
afde35469481: Pull complete
```

```
Digest: sha256:de774a3145f7ca4f0bd144c7d4ffb2931e06634f11529653
b23eba85aef8e378
Status: Downloaded newer image for ubuntu:latest
---> cd6d8154f1e1
Step 2/5 : LABEL maintainer "kijangla@example.com"
---> Running in 2d6e3abeff60
---> b7df3b688aca
Removing intermediate container 2d6e3abeff60
Step 3/5 : RUN apt-get update
---> Running in 8bd46979c5fa
```

Moving forward as part of Step 3/5, a bunch of other packages are installed as apt-get update is executed.

```
Step 3/5 : RUN apt-get update
---> Running in 8bd46979c5fa
Get:1 http://security.ubuntu.com/ubuntu bionic-security
      InRelease [83.2 kB]
Get:2 http://archive.ubuntu.com/ubuntu bionic InRelease [242 kB]
Get:3 http://security.ubuntu.com/ubuntu bionic-security/
      universe Sources [17.4 kB]
Get:4 http://archive.ubuntu.com/ubuntu bionic-updates InRelease
      [88.7 kB]
Get:5 http://security.ubuntu.com/ubuntu bionic-security/
      multiverse amd64 Packages [1363 B]
Get:6 http://security.ubuntu.com/ubuntu bionic-security/main
      amd64 Packages [203 kB]
Get:7 http://archive.ubuntu.com/ubuntu bionic-backports
      InRelease [74.6 kB]
Get:8 http://archive.ubuntu.com/ubuntu bionic/universe Sources
      [11.5 MB]
Get:9 http://security.ubuntu.com/ubuntu bionic-security/
      universe amd64 Packages [69.0 kB]
```

```
Get:10 http://archive.ubuntu.com/ubuntu bionic/main amd64
       Packages [1344 kB]
Get:11 http://archive.ubuntu.com/ubuntu bionic/universe amd64
       Packages [11.3 MB]
Get:12 http://archive.ubuntu.com/ubuntu bionic/multiverse amd64
       Packages [186 kB]
Get:13 http://archive.ubuntu.com/ubuntu bionic/restricted amd64
       Packages [13.5 kB]
Get:14 http://archive.ubuntu.com/ubuntu bionic-updates/universe
       Sources [70.4 kB]
Get:15 http://archive.ubuntu.com/ubuntu bionic-updates/universe
       amd64 Packages [226 kB]
Get:16 http://archive.ubuntu.com/ubuntu bionic-updates/main
       amd64 Packages [401 kB]
Get:17 http://archive.ubuntu.com/ubuntu bionic-updates/
       multiverse amd64 Packages [3925 B]
Get:18 http://archive.ubuntu.com/ubuntu bionic-backports/
       universe amd64 Packages [2807 B]
Fetched 25.9 MB in 3s (8072 kB/s)
Reading package lists...
---> e8081b840106
Removing intermediate container 8bd46979c5fa
```

Furthermore, Step 4/5 gets executed where the apt-get install -y nginx command runs. As a part of this run command, it builds a dependency tree and installs more packages.

```
Step 4/5 : RUN apt-get install -y nginx
---> Running in 4e8613ee2337
Reading package lists...
Building dependency tree...
Reading state information...
```

The following additional packages will be installed:
    fontconfig-config fonts-dejavu-core geoip-database
    libbsd0 libexpat1
    libfontconfig1 libfreetype6 libgd3 libgeoip1 libicu60
    libjbig0
    libjpeg-turbo8 libjpeg8 libnginx-mod-http-geoip
    libnginx-mod-http-image-filter libnginx-mod-http-xslt-
    filter
    libnginx-mod-mail libnginx-data libxau6 libxdmcp6 libxml
    libxpm4
    libxslt1.1 multiarch-support nginx-common nginx-code ucf
Suggested packages:
    Libgd-tools geoip-bin fcgiwrap nginx-doc ssl-cert
The following NEW packages will be installed:
    fontconfig-config fonts-dejavu-core geoip-database
    libbsd0 libexpat1
    libfontconfig1 libfreetype6 libgd3 libgeoip1 libicu60
    libjbig0
    libjpeg-turbo8 libjpeg8 libnginx-mod-http-geoip
    libnginx-mod-http-image-filter libnginx-mod-http-xslt-
    filter
    libnginx-mod-mail libnginx-data libxau6 libxdmcp6 libxml
    libxpm4
    libxslt1.1 multiarch-support nginx-common nginx-code ucf
    0 upgraded, 35 newly installed, 0 to remove and 8 no
    upgraded.
Need to get 16.1 MB of archives.

Soon after, it will install some additional archives.

Need to get 16.1 MB of archives
Get:1 http://security.ubuntu.com/ubuntu bionic-security
    InRelease [83.2 kB]

```
Get:2 http://archive.ubuntu.com/ubuntu bionic InRelease
       [242 kB]
Get:3 http://security.ubuntu.com/ubuntu bionic-security/
       universe Sources [17.4 kB]
Get:4 http://archive.ubuntu.com/ubuntu bionic-updates InRelease
       [88.7 kB]
Get:5 http://security.ubuntu.com/ubuntu bionic-security/
       multiverse amd64 Packages [1363 B]
Get:6 http://security.ubuntu.com/ubuntu bionic-security/main
       amd64 Packages [203 kB]
Get:7 http://archive.ubuntu.com/ubuntu bionic-backports
       InRelease [74.6 kB]
Get:8 http://archive.ubuntu.com/ubuntu bionic/universe Sources
       [11.5 MB]
Get:9 http://security.ubuntu.com/ubuntu bionic-security/
       universe amd64 Packages [69.0 kB]
Get:10 http://archive.ubuntu.com/ubuntu bionic/main amd64
       Packages [1344 kB]
Get:11 http://archive.ubuntu.com/ubuntu bionic/universe amd64
       Packages [11.3 MB]
Get:12 http://archive.ubuntu.com/ubuntu bionic/multiverse amd64
       Packages [186 kB]
Get:13 http://archive.ubuntu.com/ubuntu bionic/restricted amd64
       Packages [13.5 kB]
Get:14 http://archive.ubuntu.com/ubuntu bionic-updates/universe
       Sources [70.4 kB]
Get:15 http://archive.ubuntu.com/ubuntu bionic-updates/universe
       amd64 Packages [226 kB]
Get:16 http://archive.ubuntu.com/ubuntu bionic-updates/main
       amd64 Packages [401 kB]
Get:17 http://archive.ubuntu.com/ubuntu bionic-updates/
       multiverse amd64 Packages [3925 B]
```

```
Get:18 http://archive.ubuntu.com/ubuntu bionic-backports/
       universe amd64 Packages [2807 B]
Get:19 http://security.ubuntu.com/ubuntu bionic-security
       InRelease [83.2 kB]
Get:20 http://archive.ubuntu.com/ubuntu bionic InRelease [242 kB]
Get:21 http://security.ubuntu.com/ubuntu bionic-security/
       universe Sources [17.4 kB]
Get:22 http://archive.ubuntu.com/ubuntu bionic-updates
       InRelease [88.7 kB]
Get:23 http://security.ubuntu.com/ubuntu bionic-security/
       multiverse amd64 Packages [1363 B]
Get:24 http://security.ubuntu.com/ubuntu bionic-security/main
       amd64 Packages [203 kB]
Get:25 http://archive.ubuntu.com/ubuntu bionic-backports
       InRelease [74.6 kB]
Get:26 http://archive.ubuntu.com/ubuntu bionic/universe Sources
       [11.5 MB]
Get:27 http://security.ubuntu.com/ubuntu bionic-security/
       universe amd64 Packages [69.0 kB]
Get:28 http://archive.ubuntu.com/ubuntu bionic/main amd64
       Packages [1344 kB]
Get:29 http://archive.ubuntu.com/ubuntu bionic/universe amd64
       Packages [11.3 MB]
Get:30 http://archive.ubuntu.com/ubuntu bionic/multiverse amd64
       Packages [186 kB]
Get:31 http://archive.ubuntu.com/ubuntu bionic/restricted amd64
       Packages [13.5 kB]
Get:32 http://archive.ubuntu.com/ubuntu bionic-updates/universe
       Sources [70.4 kB]
Get:33 http://archive.ubuntu.com/ubuntu bionic-updates/universe
       amd64 Packages [226 kB]
```

```
Get:34 http://archive.ubuntu.com/ubuntu bionic-updates/main
       amd64 Packages [401 kB]
Get:35 http://archive.ubuntu.com/ubuntu bionic/main amd64 nginx
       all 1.14.0-ubuntu[3596 B]
```

It'll continue to unpack some of the installed dependencies.

```
Hit http://ppa.launchpad.net trusty InRelease
Get:1 https://ubuntu-archive.pinadmin.com trusty InRelease
Ign https://ubuntu-archive.pinadmin.com trusty InRelease
Get:2 https://artifacts.pinadmin.com trusty InRelease
Ign https://artifacts.pinadmin.com trusty InRelease
Get:3 https://puppetlabs.pinadmin.com trusty InRelease
Ign https://puppetlabs.pinadmin.com trusty InRelease
Hit https://ubuntu-archive.pinadmin.com trusty-security InRelease
Get:4 https://debrepo-trusty.pinadmin.com trusty InRelease
Hit https://download.docker.com trusty InRelease
Ign https://debrepo-trusty.pinadmin.com trusty InRelease
Hit https://saltrepo.pinadmin.com trusty InRelease
Hit https://artifacts.pinadmin.com trusty-security InRelease
Hit https://puppetlabs.pinadmin.com trusty Release.gpg
Hit https://debrepo-trusty.pinadmin.com trusty Release.gpg
Hit https://deb.nodesource.com precise InRelease
Hit https://puppetlabs.pinadmin.com trusty Release
Hit https://download.docker.com trusty/stable amd64 Packages
Hit https://debrepo-trusty.pinadmin.com trusty Release
Hit https://saltrepo.pinadmin.com trusty/main amd64 Packages
Hit https://deb.nodesource.com precise/main Sources
Hit https://deb.nodesource.com precise/main amd64 Packages
Hit https://puppetlabs.pinadmin.com trusty/puppet amd64 Packages
Hit https://debrepo-trusty.pinadmin.com trusty/main all Packages
Hit https://debrepo-trusty.pinadmin.com trusty/main amd64
Packages
```

Hit https://ubuntu-archive.pinadmin.com trusty-updates InRelease
Hit http://ppa.launchpad.net trusty/main amd64 Packages
Hit https://artifacts.pinadmin.com trusty-updates InRelease
Hit https://ubuntu-archive.pinadmin.com trusty Release.gpg
Hit https://artifacts.pinadmin.com trusty Release.gpg
Ign http://binaries.erlang-solutions.com trusty InRelease
Hit https://ubuntu-archive.pinadmin.com trusty-security/main
amd64 Packages
Hit https://artifacts.pinadmin.com trusty-security/main amd64
Packages
Hit https://ubuntu-archive.pinadmin.com trusty-security/
universe amd64 Packages
Hit http://binaries.erlang-solutions.com trusty Release.gpg
Hit https://artifacts.pinadmin.com trusty-security/restricted
amd64 Packages
Hit https://ubuntu-archive.pinadmin.com trusty-updates/main
amd64 Packages
Hit https://artifacts.pinadmin.com trusty-security/universe
amd64 Packages
Hit https://ubuntu-archive.pinadmin.com trusty-updates/universe
amd64 Packages
Hit http://binaries.erlang-solutions.com trusty Release
Hit https://artifacts.pinadmin.com trusty-updates/main amd64
Packages
Hit https://ubuntu-archive.pinadmin.com trusty Release
Hit https://artifacts.pinadmin.com trusty-updates/universe
amd64 Packages
Hit http://binaries.erlang-solutions.com trusty/contrib amd64
Packages
Hit https://ubuntu-archive.pinadmin.com trusty/main amd64
Packages
Hit https://artifacts.pinadmin.com trusty Release

```
Hit https://ubuntu-archive.pinadmin.com trusty/restricted amd64
Packages
Hit https://artifacts.pinadmin.com trusty/main amd64 Packages
Hit https://ubuntu-archive.pinadmin.com trusty/universe amd64
Packages
Hit https://artifacts.pinadmin.com trusty/restricted amd64
Packages
Hit https://artifacts.pinadmin.com trusty/universe amd64 Packages
```

It also unpacks the nginx package.

```
Reading package lists... Done
Building dependency tree
Reading state information... Done
The following packages were automatically installed and are no
longer required:
  fonts-cabin fonts-comfortaa fonts-dejavu-extra fonts-droid
  fonts-font-awesome fonts-freefont-otf fonts-gfs-artemisia
  fonts-gfs-complutum fonts-gfs-didot fonts-gfs-neohellenic
  fonts-gfs-olga
  fonts-gfs-solomos fonts-inconsolata fonts-junicode fonts-lato
  fonts-linuxlibertine fonts-lmodern fonts-lobster fonts-
  lobstertwo
  fonts-oflb-asana-math fonts-sil-gentium fonts-sil-gentium-
  basic fonts-stix
  libcupsfilters1 libcupsimage2 libfile-basedir-perl libfile-
  desktopentry-perl
  libfile-mimeinfo-perl libijs-0.35 libjbig2dec0 libkpathsea6
  libpaper-utils
  libpaper1 libpoppler44 libptexenc1 lmodern luatex pinterest-
  nginx-common
  poppler-data tcl tex-common tk ttf-adf-accanthis ttf-adf-
  gillius
```

x11-xserver-utils xdg-utils
Use 'apt-get autoremove' to remove them.
The following extra packages will be installed:
  nginx-common nginx-core
Suggested packages:
  fcgiwrap nginx-doc
The following packages will be REMOVED:
  pinterest-nginx
The following NEW packages will be installed:
  nginx nginx-common nginx-core
0 upgraded, 3 newly installed, 1 to remove and 148 not
upgraded.
Need to get 349 kB of archives.
After this operation, 6,641 kB disk space will be freed.
Get:1 https://artifacts.pinadmin.com/artifactory/ubuntu-
      archive-remote/ trusty-security/main nginx-common all
      1.4.6-1ubuntu3.8 [19.1 kB]
Get:2 https://artifacts.pinadmin.com/artifactory/ubuntu-
      archive-remote/ trusty-security/main nginx-core amd64
      1.4.6-1ubuntu3.8 [325 kB]
Get:3 https://artifacts.pinadmin.com/artifactory/ubuntu-
      archive-remote/ trusty-security/main nginx all
      1.4.6-1ubuntu3.8 [5,394 B]
Fetched 349 kB in 0s (1,887 kB/s)
Preconfiguring packages ...
(Reading database ... 168260 files and directories currently
installed.)
Removing pinterest-nginx (1.9.2) ...
Selecting previously unselected package nginx-common.
(Reading database ... 168258 files and directories currently
installed.)

```
Preparing to unpack .../nginx-common_1.4.6-1ubuntu3.8_all.deb ...
Unpacking nginx-common (1.4.6-1ubuntu3.8) ...
dpkg: error processing archive /var/cache/apt/archives/nginx-
common_1.4.6-1ubuntu3.8_all.deb (--unpack):
trying to overwrite '/lib/systemd/system/nginx.service', which
is also in package pinterest-nginx-common 1.9.2
Selecting previously unselected package nginx-core.
Preparing to unpack .../nginx-core_1.4.6-1ubuntu3.8_amd64.deb ...
Unpacking nginx-core (1.4.6-1ubuntu3.8) ...
Selecting previously unselected package nginx.
Preparing to unpack .../nginx_1.4.6-1ubuntu3.8_all.deb ...
Unpacking nginx (1.4.6-1ubuntu3.8) ...
```

It then sets up the nginx package and removes the intermediate container.

```
Debconf: falling back to frontend: Teletype
Setting up libnginx-mod-mail (1.14.0-0ubuntu1) . . .
Setting up libxdmcp6:amd64 (1:1.1.2-3) . . .
Setting up libnginx-mod-http-geoip (1.14.0-0ubuntu1) . . .
Setting up libx11-data (2:1.6.4-3) . . .
Setting up libxau6:amd64 (1:1.0.8-1) . . .
Setting up libwebp6:amd64 (0.6.1-2) . . .
Setting up libjpeg8:amd64 (8c-2ubuntu8) . . .
Setting up libnginx-mod-mail (1.14.0-0ubuntu1) . . .
Setting up libnginx-mod-http-geoip (1.14.0-0ubuntu1) . . .
Setting up libx11-data (2:1.6.4-3) . . .
Setting up libxau6:amd64 (1:1.0.8-1) . . .
Setting up libwebp6:amd64 (0.6.1-2) . . .
Setting up nginx (1.14.0-0ubuntu1) . . .
Processing triggers for libc-bin (2.27-3ubuntu1) . . .
```

```
---> 3e5c6069eaf3
Removing intermediate container 5bae8841a2ac
```

Finally, it executes the CMD command and builds the image successfully.

```
Step 5/5: CMD echo Hello World!
---> Running in 171dfcbaks42ka
---> 35c2e82eajd416
Removing intermediate container 171hsbva624bs9
Successful built 35c2e82eajd416
```

To view the image that you just built, run the command docker image ls, and you should be able to see the preceding successfully built image in the list.

```
kinnaryjangla@dev-abc:~/code/demo/docker$ docker image ls
REPOSITORY    TAG       IMAGE ID       CREATED        SIZE
Ubuntu        latest    113a43faa138   4 weeks ago    81.1MB
```

In the next section, let's run this image inside a container.

Docker Containers

Now that we have built a Docker image successfully, let's look into what a Docker container is and run this image inside a container.

As we've seen before, Docker containers provide a different form of isolation than virtual machines (VMs). They are lightweight platforms to package your entire microservices application and have it running inside the container.

Let's run inside a container the image we built successfully. There are multiple ways to run a Docker image inside a container.

In the code below, we see the image ID and the tag name of the Docker image.

```
kinnaryjangla@dev-abc:~/code/demo/docker$ docker image ls
REPOSITORY    TAG      IMAGE ID      CREATED       SIZE
Ubuntu        latest   113a43faa138  4 weeks ago   81.1MB
```

You could use either or both to run the image inside a container.

Using the name and the tag ID together, you could run the image as follows:

```
kinnaryjangla@dev-abc:~/code/demo/docker$ docker container run
-I -t ubuntu:latest /bin/bash root@cffbfc9312: /#
```

Alternatively, you could run the image as in the following, without the tag name and using only the image ID:

```
kinnaryjangla@dev-abc:~/code/demo/docker$  docker container run
-i -t 113a43faa138    /bin/bash root@cffbfc9312
```

Now, before we can see how to explore the container, let's first confirm that the container is up and running. In another window, run the `docker container ls` command, and you should be able to view the container, in the list of containers.

```
kinnaryjangla@dev-abc:~/code/demo/docker$  docker container ls
CONTAINER ID    IMAGE        COMMAND      CREATED       STATUS
PORTS                             NAMES
d121c440051b    113a43faa138 "/bin/bash"  8 seconds ago Up 7 seconds
0.0.0.0-5001->8821/tcp            dreamy_clean
```

Now let's look inside the container. Your container has the ID *1c3e3baace92*.

There are multiple ways to get inside your running container using `docker exec`, `docker attach`, etc.

```
kinnaryjangla@dev-abc:~/code/demo/docker$ docker container
attach dreamly_clean
    root@517s27n525fs: /#

kinnaryjangla@dev-abc:~/code/demo/docker$ docker container exec
-t -i dreamy_clean  /bin/bash
root@517s27n525fs: /# ls
bin   host   dev   src   home   lib   lib64   media   mnt
opt   proc   root   run   sbin   srv   sys   tmp   usr   var
root@517s27n525fs: /#
```

When inside the container, you can view logs, volumes that have been mounted, etc. Getting inside the Docker container very much comes in handy when debugging errors.

Because we started a shell, to get out of the container, just close the shell, by using the exit command, and you should be back on the command prompt of your local terminal.

```
root@517s27n525fs: /# exit
exit
kinnaryjangla@dev-abc:~/code/demo/docker$
```

Attaching and Detaching from a Docker Container

Attaching to the Docker container means attaching the local standard input/output to the Docker container. Detaching means detaching your local input/output from the Docker container. Now you'll learn how to attach to and detach from a Docker container.

In order to attach to the Docker container, first run the Docker image, and give it a name, say, "testdemo."

```
kinnaryjangla@dev-abc:~/code/demo/docker$ docker
container run -d --name testdemo ubuntu /usr/bin/tap -b
easjhf7ejbadgsvkaid888sagdhabgfks555

kinnaryjangla@dev-abv:~/code/demo/docker$
```

Next, let's attach our local terminal standard input/output to the container using docker container attach, as shown in Figure 5-1.

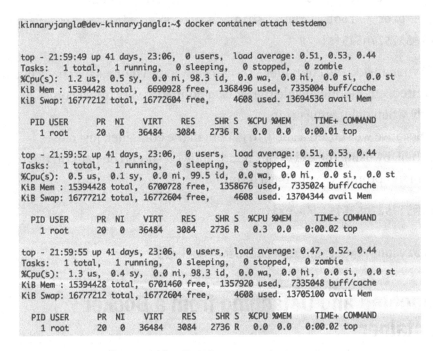

***Figure 5-1.** Attaching to the Docker container*

You should see that your terminal is now attached to the container's input/output.

Let's do another quick example, in which you can see the exit code of your container in your local terminal output.

```
kinnaryjangla@dev-abc:~/code/demo/docker$ docker container run
-name test -d -it ubuntu
easjhf7ejbadgsvkaid888sagdhabgfks555
kinnaryjangla@dev-abc:~/code/demo/docker$ docker container
attach test
root@ksjhdf6t3uqe: /# exit 13
exit
kinnaryjangla@dev-abc:~/code/demo/docker$ echo $?
13
kinnaryjangla@dev-abc:~/code/demo/docker$ docker container ls
-a | grep test
ksjhdf6t3uqe    ubuntu    "/bin/bash"    28 seconds ago
Exited(13) 15 seconds ago
```

In this example, we run the image inside a container and call it test. We then attach the container to the local standard input/output. From inside the container, we set an exit code of 13, which exits the container. On your local terminal, when you echo, you see 13 as the output. In your list of containers, you see that the container exited, owing due to the exit code 13.

You can also create a new container over a certain image. This is useful when you want to set up a container configuration beforehand.

To create a container over our Ubuntu image, let's use docker container create -t -I ubuntu bash.

```
kinnaryjangla@dev-abc:~/code/demo/docker$
docker container create -t -I ubuntu bash
cee13y299o1hkjasd462e4jhdasi7673242hbd76gdewu
```

Then start this container, using the first few letters of the container ID that was created previously.

```
kinnaryjangla@dev-abc:~/code/demo/docker$ docker container
start -a -i cee13y299
root@ cee13y299: /#
```

This lands you inside the newly created container.

You can do various things when you create a container, such as initializing volumes and even removing them using the -v option.

Now that we've looked at how to create Dockerfiles, how to build images with Dockerfiles, and how to run these images inside a container, in the next chapter, let's look at how to link multiple containers,in order to get an entire microservices application up and running on Docker.

Summary

In this chapter, we looked at what a Dockerfile is and created a basic Dockerfile step by step. You learned that a Dockerfile is the first step to anything Docker.

Later, we built an image using this Dockerfile. We looked at how to list all the images on your host machine.

Later, we ran this image inside a container and looked at how to attach the container to our local terminal input/output. We executed a few examples and attached and detached the container to our local terminal. You also learned how to list all the containers that are up and running on your machine.

In the next chapter, we'll look at how to link multiple containers, hence multiple services to each other, and create a real-world microservices application, using Docker.

CHAPTER 6

Docker Compose

Composition: "the act of combining parts or elements to form a whole."

Dictionary.com, s.v. "composition,"
www.dictionary.com/browse/composition, accessed October 2, 2018.

In the previous chapter, we studied Dockerfiles and Docker images, how to build images, and run them in Docker containers. But if you think about practical day-to-day workflows, they are seldom going to occur on a single service. A workflow is usually a composition of multiple services or microservices. So, in order to get an application running on Docker from end to end, you have to link multiple Docker containers running different services, in such a way that they can talk to one another.

In this chapter, you'll see how we can get multiple Docker containers running different services up and running simultaneously and efficiently, in order to get an end-to-end application up and running, using Docker.

What Is Docker Compose

In the previous chapters, you saw the advantages of running services on Docker containers. Some of the advantages are consistent environment variables, isolation of dependencies, and enabling continuous deployment of these services.

© Kinnary Jangla 2018
K. Jangla, *Accelerating Development Velocity Using Docker*,
https://doi.org/10.1007/978-1-4842-3936-0_6

Today, most software applications are made of multiple services that talk to each other. In order to make such applications operational, you have to link several Docker containers to one another and have them all running simultaneously on Docker in production. Let's see how we can link multiple Docker containers.

Docker Compose is the tool for running multi-container Docker applications. It's essentially a YAML file that can be thought of as a composition of multiple Dockerfile containers running commands into a single file. This Docker compose YAML file contains configurations of multiple services. Then, using a single command, you can get all the services up and running simultaneously inside Docker containers.

You can also configure these services in such a way that they talk to each other.

So, Docker Compose requires you to do the following three things:

1. Define the configuration of the running container inside a Dockerfile.

2. Create a Docker Compose YAML file that contains configurations of all the services you want up and running.

3. Then run the command `docker-compose up`, which runs the YAML file and your entire application.

Docker Compose can be used to create this microservices architecture and link the containers between them, or it can be used for a single service. In addition, Docker Compose can build images, scale containers, and rerun stopped containers. All this functionality is a part of Docker. `docker-compose` is just a higher-level abstraction of container `run` commands. You can do everything you can in a compose file with plain Docker commands, except that this requires more memory and takes extra effort to run all the extra commands, attaching to the network, etc. `docker-compose` helps to simplify this process.

Let's look at a sample Docker Compose YAML file, as shown following:

```
version: '3'
services:
  myapp:
    build: .
    ports:
      - "5001:8887"
    command: "bash scripts/local_test_server.sh"
    container_name: myApp
    volumes:
      - "/home/{{USER}}/code/services/myApp:/var/src/myApp"
      - "/var/serverset:/var/serverset"
      - "/var/config:/var/config"
    environment:
      - HEAP_SIZE=4G
      - CLASSPATH=/code/services/myApp-0.1-SNAPSHOT

  redis:
    image: "redis:alpine"
    ports:
      - "5001:9020"
    command: "bash scripts/run_in_container.sh"
    container_name: redis
    volumes:
      - "/home/{{USER}}/code/redis:/var/src/redis"
      - "/var/serverset:/var/serverset"
      - "/var/config:/var/config"
    environment:
      - HEAP_SIZE=4G
```

```
networks:
  default:
    driver: my-driver-1
```

In this example, the Docker Compose YAML file has configurations for two services, namely, myApp and Redis, wherein myApp is an application service and Redis is a database. Let's look at what some of the fields in the YAML file represent. First, the Docker Compose YAML file tells Docker to build the images for the services—myApp and Redis. The `build` instruction asks to look for the file `Dockerfile-dev` in the folder myApp.

Instead of using the `build` key, you could specify the image. If you use image, specify the image name. This pulls up the specific image.

Next, the `ports` instruction indicates to map port 5001 on the host to the service1 docker containers port 8887.

The `command` instruction specifies the first command to run, in order to get the service up and running.

`container_name` is intuitive. It specifies the name of the Docker container in which myApp will run. This is used to identify which services run inside which Docker container. However, most compose files do not define the container name. Names must be unique. Once you specify a name, you have removed the ability to scale the number of replicas used for a service. When the `docker-compose` tool starts the container without a specified name, the generated name helps to identify the service.

The `volumes` instructions let you map certain files and folders on the host machine to the Docker container. For example, `/home/{{USER}}/code/services/service1:/var/src/myApp` says to map the folder `code/services/service1` to the folder `var/src/myApp` on the Docker container. This command is very useful when debugging inside the Docker container, so that you can use the files that exist on the host machine.

The `environment` instruction basically configures the environment variables for the services.

The networks key lets you define a network that each service wants to connect to. You can also specify a default network that can be used for the entire app. If there is an existing network that you want the containers to join, you can employ the external option.

In addition to the instructions in the preceding sample Docker Compose YAML file, you could use deploy to specify the deployment specifications, such as the number of replicas, resources, CPU, and memory limits on these resources, restart policies, etc. The deploy key only applies when deploying to a Swarm. We'll look at that in more detail in later chapters.

Next let's see how to install Docker Compose on your machine.

Installing Docker Compose

Docker Compose relies on the Docker Engine, so before you install Compose, make sure you have Docker installed on your machine.

The Docker Desktop tool includes the docker-compose tool.

In order to get Docker for a Mac system, refer to the "Installing Docker" section in Chapter 4. For older machines, you can get the Docker Toolbox. Docker Toolbox helps you quickly set up and install the Docker environment on your Mac or Windows machine. Docker Toolbox includes docker-machine, docker, docker-compose, Docker GUIs, and Docker CLIs.

You can uninstall Docker Compose in two ways, unless you've installed the Docker Compose tool with Docker Desktop. In this case, you'll have to uninstall Docker Desktop.

It's quick and easy to install Docker Compose using curl. If you've installed it using curl, you can uninstall it using the following command:

```
sudo rm /usr/local/bin/docker-compose
```

If you installed Docker Compose using `pip`, you can uninstall it using this command:

```
pip uninstall docker-compose
```

Usage

Let's look at some basic Docker Compose commands.

docker-compose up

The main command to keep in mind when using Docker Compose is `docker-compose up`. This command gets all your services running per the specified configuration in your Docker Compose YAML file.

Usage:

```
up [options] [--scale SERVICE=NUM...] [SERVICE...]
```

You can use this command with multiple options, such as the following:

> `-d` or `--detach`: This allows you to run Docker Compose in detached mode, which means running containers in the background.

> `--quiet-pull`: This pulls the images without printing progress information.

> `--no-deps`: This instructs the system not to start the linking services.

> `--build`: This builds the images before starting the containers.

> `--remove-orphans`: This removes all the other containers not specified in this `docker-compose` YAML file.

docker-compose build

This command allows you to build all the services in the YAML file, after which all the images built are tagged with the image name. If you change the service's Dockerfile, make sure to set docker-compose build again, in order to build the new image.

Usage:

```
build [options] [--build-arg key=val...] [SERVICE...]
```

Some options to use with this command are

- -compress: This compresses the build using gzip.

- -force-rm: Remove intermediate containers at all times.

- -no-cache: Disable use of cache when building the image.

- -pull: Pull the newer version of the image, if it exists.

docker-compose config

It's a great idea to validate your Docker Compose config file once you've created one. This command can be used for that.

Usage:

```
config [options]
```

Some options to use with this command are

- -q, - -quiet: Validate without printing anything.

- -services: Print services name, one per line.

- -volumes: Print volume names, one per line.

docker-compose kill

This command forces all running commands to stop, by sending the SIGKILL signal.

Usage:

```
kill [options] [SERVICE...]
```

docker-compose restart

This command restarts all the services that have been previously stopped or are currently running.

Usage:

```
restart [options] [SERVICE...]
```

You can use the timeout option with this command, using -t or --timeout.

docker-compose ps

This command lists all the containers that were successfully started.

Usage:

```
ps [options] [SERVICE...]
```

docker-compose logs

This command outputs the logs from all services.

Usage:

```
logs [options] [SERVICE...]
```

Some options to use with this command are

-f, - -follow: Follow the output of the logs.

- -t, - -timestamps: Display the timestamps.

- -tail="all": The number of lines from the end
of the logs that you want displayed for each Docker
container.

docker-compose start

This command starts existing containers for all services.
Usage:

```
start [SERVICE...]
```

docker-compose stop

This command stops running containers but does not remove them. You
can restart containers using docker-compose start.
Usage:

```
stop [options] [SERVICE...]
```

docker-compose pause

This command pauses the running services. They can be unpaused using
docker-compose unpause.
Usage:

```
pause [SERVICE...]
```

docker-compose run

This command runs a command once for a particular service that is specified with the command.

Usage:

```
run [options] [-v VOLUME...] [-p PORT...] [-e KEY=VAL...]
      SERVICE [COMMAND] [ARGS...]
```

For example, `docker-compose run service1 bash` starts the service `service1` and runs `bash` as its command.

Some options you can use with this command are

   `-d, - -detach`: Run the container in the background.

   `- -name NAME`: Assign a name to the container.

   `- -entrypoint CMD`: Override the given entry point of that image.

   `- -e KEY=VAL`: Set an environment variable called `KEY` and assign it the value `VAL`.

   `- -u, - -user`: Run as a specified user.

   `- -rm`: Remove the container after the run is over.

When you run `docker-compose run`, the commands used with `run` start new Docker containers with configurations specified with that command in the options. It is important to note that the commands passed along with the `run` command override the configuration in the Docker Compose YAML file. Another important thing to note is that the `docker-compose run` command creates or uses any of the ports specified in the Docker Compose YAML file, in order to avoid port collisions. If you want to specify a port, you can use the `- -service-ports` flag in your `docker-compose run` command.

Now that we've looked at some basic `docker-compose` usages, let's look at what's really happening behind the scenes of Docker Compose.

Behind the Scenes and an Example

In the previous chapters, you saw how a single Dockerfile can be built into a single Docker image. Similar to that, a single Docker Compose YAML file can be built into a stack of images. This stack is also called a distributed application bundle (DAB).

Docker stacks and Docker bundles are features in Docker and Docker Compose.

The simplest way to create a Docker bundle is via Docker Compose. Using `docker-compose bundle` builds all the images of the services in the YAML file and creates a bundle. In order to deploy this bundle, you have to create a Docker stack. This can be done using `docker deploy`. You can manage this stack using the `docker stack` command.

Further, let's work through a simple `docker-compose` example in which we will link two services.

As a first step, let's create a directory called `test`, then change into that directory.

```
kinnaryjangla@dev-abc:~/code$ mkdir test
kinnaryjangla@dev-abc:~/code$ cd test
kinnaryjangla@dev-abc:~/code/test$
```

Next, create a file called `myapp.py` in the `test` directory and paste this content into it:

```
import time

import redis
from flask import Flask

app = Flask(__name__)
cache = redis.Redis(host='redis', port=6379)
```

```
def get_page_count():
    retries = 3
    while True:
        try:
            return cache.incr('hits')
        except redis.exceptions.ConnectionError as exc:
            if retries == 0:
                raise exc
            retries -= 1
            time.sleep(0.5)

@app.route('/')
def helloWorld():
    count = get_page_count()
    return 'Hello World! You have been here {} times.\n'.
    format(count)

if __name__ == "__main__":
    app.run(host="0.0.0.0", debug=True)
```

In this example, redis refers to the Redis Docker container, and we use 6379, which is the default port for Redis.

Note that Flask and Redis are requirements for this file. So, next, create a requirements.txt file in the test directory and paste in the following:

```
flask
redis
```

As a next step, let's create a Dockerfile for this service. Create a file called Dockerfile in your test project directory and paste in the following:

```
FROM python:3.4-alpine
WORKDIR /code
```

```
ADD . /code
RUN pip install -r requirements.txt
CMD ["python", "myapp.py"]
```

Let's look at what the instructions in this Dockerfile mean. The FROM instruction pulls the alpine image from the Docker registry and builds the image. Next, the ADD instruction says to add the current directory . into the /code directory in the image. The WORKDIR command sets the working directory in the container to /code. The RUN instruction installs the Python dependencies, namely, Flask and Redis, as defined in the requirements. txt file. The CMD instruction then sets the default command for the Docker container to python myapp.py.

So now that we have the Dockerfile for our service created, let's start a Redis service that our app can talk to that pulls an existing Redis image from the Docker registry. In practice, this could be replaced by another similar service to that we created previously.

Let's create a file called docker-compose.yml in our test project directory. Then paste in this:

```
version: '3'
services:
  myapp:
    build: .
    ports:
     - "5000:5000"
  redis:
    image: "redis:alpine"
```

This is made up of two services, one of which is defined by us, called myapp, that is built by the Dockerfile in the current project directory. This configuration maps the port 5000 on the host machine to the port 5000 on the Docker container running this service. The other service is Redis, which pulls an existing Redis image from the default Docker Hub registry.

From your project directory, now run docker-compose up.
You should see the following:

1. First, it pulls the Python 3.4 image to build the image
   we specified in the earlier Dockerfile.

```
kinnaryjangla@dev-abc:~/code/test$ docker-compose up
Creating network "test_default" with the default driver
Pulling redis (redis:alpine)...
alpine: Pulling from library/redis
8e3ba11ec2a2: Pull complete
1f20bd2a5c23: Pull complete
782ff7702b5c: Pull complete
82d1d664c6a7: Pull complete
69f8979cc310: Pull complete
3ff30b3bc148: Pull complete
Digest: sha256:43e4d14fcffa05a5967c353dd7061564f130d602
1725dd219f0c6fcbcc6b5076
Status: Downloaded newer image for redis:alpine
Building myapp
Step 1/5 : FROM python:3.4-alpine
3.4-alpine: Pulling from library/python
8e3ba11ec2a2: Already exists
4001a9c615cb: Pull complete
5bbb3a9b8d5e: Pull complete
5adcac484e5a: Pull complete
ffd089d04f72: Pull complete
Digest: sha256:9ecfc28113e3e0299e82fbfbbf37851b9c84efbf
931eae22ccd69d2ad1562c91
Status: Downloaded newer image for python:3.4-alpine
---> 0c5cb9a7cbd2
Step 2/5 : ADD . /code
---> 494ffafb0dbd
```

```
Removing intermediate container 56496ef21df6
Step 3/5 : WORKDIR /code
---> 3fee363b7d90
Removing intermediate container 08dc071a5e33
```

2. Next, it installs Flask and Redis, per the
   requirements specified in the requirements.txt
   file.

```
Step 4/5 : RUN pip install -r requirements.txt
---> Running in 4f3c397dedd1
Collecting flask (from -r requirements.txt (line 1))
  Downloading https://files.pythonhosted.org/packages/
  7f/e7/08578774ed4536d3242b14dacb4696386634607af824ea9
  97202cd0edb4b/Flask-1.0.2-py2.py3-none-any.whl (91kB)
Collecting redis (from -r requirements.txt (line 2))
  Downloading https://files.pythonhosted.org/packages/3b/
  f6/7a76333cf0b9251ecf49efff635015171843d9b977e4ffcf59f
  9c4428052/redis-2.10.6-py2.py3-none-any.whl (64kB)
Collecting Jinja2>=2.10 (from flask->-r requirements.
txt (line 1))
  Downloading https://files.pythonhosted.org/packages/
  7f/ff/ae64bacdfc95f27a016a7bed8e8686763ba4d277a78
  ca76f32659220a731/Jinja2-2.10-py2.py3-none-any.whl
  (126kB)
Collecting click>=5.1 (from flask->-r requirements.txt
(line 1))
  Downloading https://files.pythonhosted.org/
  packages/34/c1/8806f99713ddb993c5366c362b2f908f18269
  f8d792aff1abfd700775a77/click-6.7-py2.py3-none-any.
  whl (71kB)
Collecting itsdangerous>=0.24 (from flask->-r
requirements.txt (line 1))
```

```
    Downloading https://files.pythonhosted.org/packages/
    dc/b4/a60bcdba945c00f6d608d8975131ab3f25b22f2bcfe1
    dab221165194b2d4/itsdangerous-0.24.tar.gz (46kB)
Collecting Werkzeug>=0.14 (from flask->-r requirements.
txt (line 1))
    Downloading https://files.pythonhosted.org/packages/
    20/c4/12e3e56473e52375aa29c4764e70d1b8f3efa6682bef8d0
    aae04fe335243/Werkzeug-0.14.1-py2.py3-none-any.whl
    (322kB)
Collecting MarkupSafe>=0.23 (from Jinja2>=2.10->flask-
>-r requirements.txt (line 1))
    Downloading https://files.pythonhosted.org/packages/
    4d/de/32d741db316d8fdb7680822dd37001ef7a448255de9699
    ab4bfcbdf4172b/MarkupSafe-1.0.tar.gz
Building wheels for collected packages:
itsdangerous, MarkupSafe
    Running setup.py bdist_wheel for itsdangerous:
started
    Running setup.py bdist_wheel for itsdangerous:
    finished with status 'done'
    Stored in directory: /root/.cache/pip/
    wheels/2c/4a/61/5599631c1554768c6290b08c02c72d7317910
    374ca602ff1e5
    Running setup.py bdist_wheel for MarkupSafe: started
    Running setup.py bdist_wheel for MarkupSafe: finished
    with status 'done'
    Stored in directory: /root/.cache/pip/
    wheels/33/56/20/
    ebe49a5c612fffe1c5a632146b16596f9e64676768661e4e46
Successfully built itsdangerous MarkupSafe
Installing collected packages: MarkupSafe, Jinja2,
click, itsdangerous, Werkzeug, flask, redis
```

Successfully installed Jinja2-2.10 MarkupSafe-1.0
Werkzeug-0.14.1 click-6.7 flask-1.0.2 itsdangerous-0.24
redis-2.10.6
---> a8a506f87306
Removing intermediate container 4f3c397dedd1

3. Finally, it executes the last instruction and runs the
   Python myapp.py command.

```
Step 5/5 : CMD python myapp.py
---> Running in c2113e2877dc
---> 104b362fbe0b
Removing intermediate container c2113e2877dc
Successfully built 104b362fbe0b
Successfully tagged test_myapp:latest
WARNING: Image for service myapp was built because it did
not already exist. To rebuild this image you must use
`docker-compose build` or `docker-compose up --build`.
Creating test_myapp_1 ...
Creating test_redis_1 ...
Creating test_redis_1
Creating test_redis_1 ... done
Attaching to test_myapp_1, test_redis_1
redis_1  | 1:C 01 Sep 21:04:35.245 # o000o000o0000o
Redis is starting o000o000o0000o
redis_1  | 1:C 01 Sep 21:04:35.245 # Redis
version=4.0.11, bits=64, commit=00000000, modified=0,
pid=1, just started
redis_1  | 1:C 01 Sep 21:04:35.245 # Warning: no config
file specified, using the default config. In order to
specify a config file use redis-server /path/to/redis.conf
redis_1  | 1:M 01 Sep 21:04:35.246 * Running
mode=standalone, port=6379.
```

```
redis_1  | 1:M 01 Sep 21:04:35.247 # WARNING: The TCP
backlog setting of 511 cannot be enforced because /
proc/sys/net/core/somaxconn is set to the lower value
of 128.
redis_1  | 1:M 01 Sep 21:04:35.247 # Server initialized
redis_1  | 1:M 01 Sep 21:04:35.247 # WARNING
overcommit_memory is set to 0! Background save may
fail under low memory condition. To fix this issue add
'vm.overcommit_memory = 1' to /etc/sysctl.conf and
then reboot or run the command 'sysctl vm.overcommit_
memory=1' for this to take effect.
redis_1  | 1:M 01 Sep 21:04:35.247 * Ready to accept
connections
myapp_1  | * Serving Flask app "myapp" (lazy loading)
myapp_1  | * Environment: production
myapp_1  |   WARNING: Do not use the development
             server in a production environment.
myapp_1  |   Use a production WSGI server instead.
myapp_1  | * Debug mode: on
myapp_1  | * Running on http://0.0.0.0:5000/
             (Press CTRL+C to quit)
myapp_1  | * Restarting with stat
myapp_1  | * Debugger is active!
myapp_1  | * Debugger PIN: 310-933-049
```

As you see from the preceding code, both services have started and are running.

Next, look at our browser. On your browser, navigate to http://0.0.0.0:5000/, to see your application running, as shown in Figure 6-1. The web app should now be listening to the port 5000 on your Docker daemon.

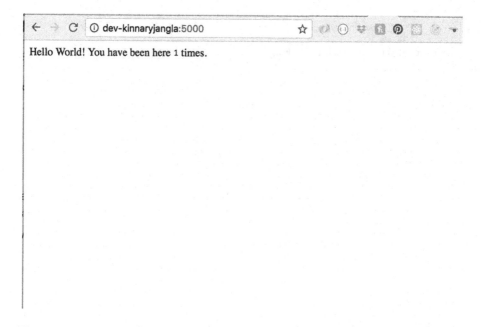

Figure 6-1. Sample application being tested on the browser

If you refresh the page, you should see the count increase from 1 to 2, as shown in Figure 6-2.

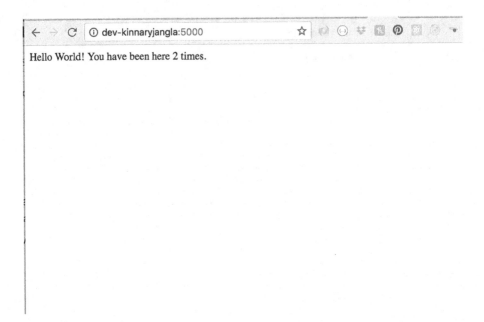

Figure 6-2. Sample application count increasing to 2

If you notice the terminal where you can see the services ready to accept connection requests, you'll see the HTTP requests on that terminal window, as follows.

```
myapp_1    |    * Serving Flask app "myapp" (lazy loading)
myapp_1    |    * Environment production
myapp_1    |      WARNING: Do not use the development server
                  in a production environment.
myapp_1    |      Use a production WSGI server instead.
myapp_1    |    * Debug mode: on
myapp_1    |    * Running on http://0.0.0.0:5000/
                  (Press STRL+C to quit)
myapp_1    |    * Restarting with stat
myapp_1    |    * Debugger is active!
```

```
myapp_1      |      * Debugger PIN: 333-632-146
myapp_1      |      172.16.8.199 - - [14/Jul/2018 23.56:30]
                    "GET /  HTTP/1.1" 200 -
myapp_1      |      172.16.8.199 - - [14/Jul/2018 23.56:39] "GET
                    /  HTTP/1.1" 200 -
```

In a different terminal window, run docker-compose ps, to see the list of running containers, as shown following.

```
kinnaryjangla@dev-abc~/code/test$ docker container ps
CONTAINER ID IMAGE COMMAND CREATED STATUS
PORTS NAMES
d121c440051b test_myapp "bash scripts/loca..." 3 hours ago Up
20 seconds
0.0.0.0-5000->5001/tcp test_myapp_1
c7f77318fa0c redis:alpine "bash scripts/loca..." 3 hours ago Up
10 seconds
6379/tcp    test/redis_1
```

Now that you've seen a running example of docker-compose, let's conclude this section.

Summary

In this chapter, we looked at Docker Compose and its uses. We saw that Docker containers running different services can be linked to one another using docker-compose.

You saw how to install and uninstall the docker-compose tool and different uses for docker-compose. Next, you saw how docker-compose creates container images and spins them. I walked you through a real-world example of Docker Compose. We created a Dockerfile for a service and a docker-compose file that links that service to a Redis image that we pulled from the Docker Hub registry. We went through how to build it and run the entire application. We looked at the browser, to see the application in action and then viewed the Docker containers running the two services that the application is composed of.

In the next chapter, I'll go through a real-world example of how to debug a real-world application composed of microservices, using Docker.

CHAPTER 7

Debugging Microservices Using Docker

Debugging is the art of identifying and removing errors from computer software.

In the previous chapter, you learned how to use and install Docker Compose and saw some examples of how to use it in real-world scenarios. You also saw what happens behind the scenes of Docker Compose when containers talk to each other.

In this chapter, you'll learn how to debug these microservices that run together with the help of Docker Compose. We'll look at the challenges of a distributed system and how we can use Docker to overcome some of the challenges related to debugging, which, in turn, can help accelerate the pace at which an engineer can develop.

In Chapter 3, we explored the differences between monolith and microservices architecture. We also looked at the challenges of a microservices architecture. A microservices architecture inherits challenges of a distributed environment. Let's look at that more closely.

© Kinnary Jangla 2018
K. Jangla, *Accelerating Development Velocity Using Docker*,
https://doi.org/10.1007/978-1-4842-3936-0_7

Distributed Environments

What exactly is a distributed system? In the simplest terms, it is a group of individual computers working together and appearing to the external user as one system. These computers have shared state, concurrency behaviors, and failure handing properties, if implemented correctly.

Some of the obvious advantages of a distributed system are sharing, collaboration, scalability, reliability, and availability. The World Wide Web is a fantastic example of a distributed system.

Advantages of Distributed Systems

Scalability

Every project starts small. As it progresses successfully, it must be expanded in several dimensions, including space, network bandwidth, CPU resources, database size, etc. The simplest solution is to replace your computers with bigger and more powerful CPUs. This is however, very inefficient, because you are throwing away previous resources, and future scalability is not taken into account.

The ideal solution is to add resources as a product grows. This is where a distributed system enables scaling very easily and more efficiently.

There are two types of scaling methods, namely, horizontal and vertical scaling. In horizontal scaling, you add more machines, and in vertical scaling, you add more resources, such as memory, CPUs, etc.

Reliability and Availability

A single point of failure can bring an entire web site down. If the application is architected correctly, however, when multiple services are running independently on different servers in a distributed system, other web sites continue running, and a single failure in the site doesn't necessarily cause system shutdown.

Autonomy

Data sharing in a distributed system allows sites to access data residing at other sites, and, at the same time, sharing data lets each site maintain a certain degree of control over the data that is stored locally. Local database administrators can then have complete autonomy to decide how to operate the databases.

For these reasons, distributed systems really shine in today's business settings. But designing a distributed system comes with its own set of challenges and is not as straightforward and simple.

Challenges of Distributed Systems

Let's look at some of the major challenges you'll face with distributed systems.

Heterogeneity

One of the advantages of distributed systems is that different components and services can be written using different tech stacks. This gives the developers the independence to use the platforms they are most comfortable with.

But when services are written in different languages, on different operating systems (OSs), use different network protocols and hardware devices, programs cannot communicate with each other, unless some common standards are established. For example, different languages use different ways of representing characters and data structures. In order for services written in different languages to communicate, this difference must somehow be bridged.

For this reason, some kind of a middleware layer must be present, to bridge the gaps of different platforms, at the same time masking the heterogeneity of everything that is underlying. Some ways of doing this are standardizing around REST or gRPC (a remote procedure call initially developed by Google).

Concealing the Complexity

As discussed, a distributed system has lot of underlying complexity, such as differences in data representation, accessibility and location of resources, resource sharing by several components, failure and recovery of resources, etc. These complexities are best masked from the user, so that the system is perceived as a single system, rather than as a set of independent components.

Concurrency

One of the advantages of a distributed system is that services and applications can access common resources. With this sharing of data comes the possibility of multiple services that can attempt to access the same resources at the same time. So, in such a scenario, objects must be able to operate efficiently in a synchronous fashion, while maintaining data consistency. This is usually achieved by using standard concurrency techniques, such as semaphores. For example, in the digital stock market, multiple people buy and sell at a single point in time.

Scalability

For a growing product, a distributed system has to scale efficiently, in order to address issues such as increasing network bandwidth; an increase in latency, which could potentially be a result of an increase in user traffic; increase in data read and writes; the number of resources to be processed;

overloading of servers; etc. For all these reasons, scaling distributed systems efficiently is a very important issue that companies such as Amazon and Google continuously work to address.

Failure Handling

Single points of failure can bring a whole system down, as previously mentioned. Having an entire service fail is extremely harmful for service availability. But we can worry about this a little less with a distributed system, because individual components can continue to operate. However, partial failures are very common in distributed systems. For example, a switch failure can interfere with some nodes of communication but not others; some network messages may be lost; some nodes crash, while some continue running. Handling of these failures is particularly difficult in a distributed system. Conversely, in a single monolith system, it is simpler to tell which process has died or exited. In a distributed system, the only way to know this is to notice a halt in receiving signals from a previously operating node. This could be difficult to debug as well, because it could either be a fatal signal or a delayed response over the network. Furthermore, it could even produce incorrect results or incomplete results. Diagnosing such issues incorrectly could cause us to come to the wrong conclusion and, thereby, lead us to solving the wrong problem.

Debugging

Given that a distributed system has multiple services linked to one another, handling of failures as those mentioned previously can get tricky. Debugging these failures can get even trickier. In order to debug, you would have to get all the services up and running first. Consider multiple services dependent of different versions of a library. Getting these services running on a single machine would be pretty difficult, maybe even impossible, without the use of some kind of virtualization.

Sample Real-World End-to-End Use Case

Some of the challenges of a distributed environment can be addressed with Docker. Let's look at how to specifically debug an end-to-end application whose service runs using Docker Compose.

Consider a web site that takes a list of interests as user input and renders images in the user's feed, based on these interests. This can get extremely complex, if you take user signals into account. That would include learning from user signals and rendering images from the categories or interests that the user is known to click most and rendering fewer images from categories or interests that the user has not clicked very often. This can become complicated very quickly. For the purpose of maintaining simplicity, I will not take user signals into account in this example.

So, let's look at what our application does. Our application basically contains a table from which user ID is mapped to a list of interests and an inverted index of interests to images in a MySQL database. When the user logs into his or her account, an HTTP request is made to a service, in order to retrieve the user's list of interests. This list is then sent to another service, which in turn looks at the database and gets five images per interest from the interest list. Once this data is returned, this service then sorts this image list according to those most recently created and sends it back to the client in the HTTP response.

This means, our application is made of three services.

1. A service that makes the HTTP request with the user ID. We will call this service Client.

2. A service that calls the MySQL database to get a list of interests for the user ID. Let's call this service DB.

3. A service that takes a list of interests as input and makes a call to the MySQL database to get a list of five images for each of those interests. When it receives the results, this service sorts these images, based on the ones most recently created, and returns them back to the Client service. Let's call this service Api.

I will not go into detail about how each service does its job or the schema of the database. For the purposes of this example, we'll look at the Dockerfiles of each service, the Docker Compose file that will get all these services up and running at the same time, and, finally, we'll make an HTTP request to our service and look at the response received and the images rendered.

Let's begin. We'll call our application FunFeed. Figure 7-1 shows how it will look.

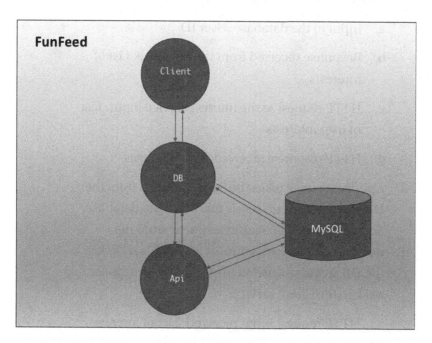

Figure 7-1. *FunFeed application, with its microservices, namely, Client, DB, and Api, and the MySQL database*

Now let's clarify the roles of all three services.

1. Client: When the user logs in to the FunFeed application, this service makes an HTTP request to the DB service with the user ID in the request and awaits a response from the DB service.

   a. HTTP request input: User ID

   b. HTTP response received: List of images to be rendered on the browser

2. DB: This service accepts the HTTP request from the Client service, takes the user ID as input, and makes a database request to get a list of interests for that user ID. It then sends this list of interests to the Api service and awaits a response.

   a. Input to the database: User ID

   b. Response received from the database: List of interests

   c. HTTP request to the interest service input: List of user interests

   d. HTTP response received: List of images

3. Api: This service takes the list of interests from the DB service as input, sends this list to the database, and gets a list of images in response from the database. It then sorts this list and sends it back to the DB service, which in turn sends this response back to the Client service.

   a. HTTP request input received: List of interests

   b. Request to database: List of interests

    c.   Response from database: List of images

    d.   Response to DB service: List of images

Now let's take a closer look at the Client service.

As mentioned, this service logs the user in and sends the user ID to the DB service (Figure 7-2).

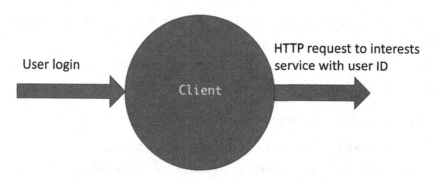

Figure 7-2.   *Client service input/output*

Let's look at the Dockerfile for the Client service.

```
# Refer https://docs.docker.com/engine/userguide/eng-image/
dockerfile_best-practices/
# for best practices maintaining this file

# Base image from https://phabricator.pinadmin.com/diffusion/
BDI
FROM openjdk:7

# Default environment variables required to run service, can be
overridden by docker run
ENV CONFIG_FILE=config/client.dev.properties \
    HEAP_SIZE=4G \
    LOG4J_CONFIG_FILE=config/log4j.dev.properties \
    NEW_SIZE=2G \
    JAVA_COMMAND=java
```

```
# Create and set current directory
WORKDIR /opt/client

# Add the build artifact under /opt, can be overridden by
docker build
ARG ARTIFACT_PATH=target/client-server-0.1-SNAPSHOT-bin.tar.gz
ADD $ARTIFACT_PATH /opt/client/

# Default command to run service, do not override it in docker
run unless have a good reason
# Use "docker logs ID" to view stdout and stderr
CMD ["scripts/run_in_container.sh"]
```

Let's look at the instructions of this Dockerfile.

1. The FROM command sets the base image for the rest of the instructions. In this case, we set the base image to openjdk:7.

2. The ENV instruction sets the environment variables for the container. In this case, we set our config file to config/client.dev.properties, our heap size to 4G, our logs config file to config/log4j.dev. properties, and our Java command to java.

3. Next, we set our working directory inside the container to /opt/client, using the WORKDIR instruction. This means when you log in to your container, you will be inside the opt/client folder.

4. With the ADD instruction, we copy the folders to the container. First, we set the argument ARTIFACT_PATH to target/client-server-0.1-SNAPSHOT-bin.tar. gz, using the ARG instruction, and next we copy this client-server-0.1-SNAPSHOT-bin.tar.gz file to the /opt/client folder inside the container.

5. And, finally, we use the CMD instruction, which
   specifies the command for the image and does
   not execute it during build time. In this case,
   the command for the image is scripts/run_in_
   container.sh. This means, that this script run_in_
   container.sh, is used to get the Client service up
   and running.

Put succinctly, the Client service Dockerfile sets the base image that
the rest of the instructions can sit on, sets some environment variables for
the client container, sets a working directory and copies some files, and,
finally, sets up the command for the image run.

Next, let's look at the Dockerfile for DB.

```
# Refer https://docs.docker.com/engine/userguide/eng-image/
dockerfile_best-practices/
# for best practices maintaining this file

# Base image from https://phabricator.pinadmin.com/diffusion/BDI
FROM openjdk:7

# Default environment variables required to run service, can be
overridden by docker run
ENV CONFIG_FILE=config/db.dev.properties \
    HEAP_SIZE=4G \
    LOG4J_CONFIG_FILE=config/log4j.dev.properties \
    NEW_SIZE=2G \
    JAVA_COMMAND=java

# Create and set current directory
WORKDIR /opt/db
```

```
# Add the build artifact under /opt, can be overridden by
docker build
ARG ARTIFACT_PATH=target/db-server-0.1-SNAPSHOT-bin.tar.gz
ADD $ARTIFACT_PATH /opt/db/

ADD target target
ADD scripts scripts
ADD config config

# Default command to run service, do not override it in docker
run unless have a good reason
# Use "docker logs ID" to view stdout and stderr
CMD ["scripts/run_in_container.sh"]
```

Let's take a look at the instructions of the DB Dockerfile.

1. The FROM command sets the base image for the rest of the instructions. In this case, we set the base image to openjdk:7.

2. The ENV instruction sets the environment variables for the container. In this case, we set our config file to config/db.yaml, our heap size to 4G, our logs config file to config/log4j.dev.properties.

3. Next, we set our working directory inside the container to /opt/db, using the WORKDIR instruction. This means when you log in to your container, you will be inside the opt/db folder.

4. With the ADD instruction, we copy the folders to the container. First, we set the argument ARTIFACT_ PATH to target/db-0.1-SNAPSHOT-bin.tar.gz, using the ARG instruction, and next we copy this db-0.1-SNAPSHOT-bin.tar.gz file to the /opt/db

folder inside the container. We also copy the target, scripts, and config folders on the host machine to the target, scripts, and config folders inside the container.

5. And, finally, we use the CMD instruction, which specifies the command for the image and does not execute it during build time. In this case, the command for the image is scripts/run_in_ container.sh. This means, that this script, run_in_ container.sh, is used to get the DB service up and running.

Next, let's take a look at the Dockerfile for the Api service.

```
# Refer https://docs.docker.com/engine/userguide/eng-image/
dockerfile_best-practices/
# for best practices maintaining this file

# Base image from https://phabricator.pinadmin.com/diffusion/BDI
FROM openjdk:7

# Default environment variables required to run service, can be
overridden by docker run
ENV CONFIG_FILE=config/api.dev.properties \
    HEAP_SIZE=4G \
    LOG4J_CONFIG_FILE=config/log4j.dev.properties \
    NEW_SIZE=2G \
    JAVA_COMMAND=java

# Create and set current directory
WORKDIR /opt/api
```

```
# Add the build artifact under /opt, can be overridden by
docker build
ARG ARTIFACT_PATH=target/api-server-0.1-SNAPSHOT-bin.tar.gz
ADD $ARTIFACT_PATH /opt/api/
```

```
# Default command to run service, do not override it in docker
run unless have a good reason
# Use "docker logs ID" to view stdout and stderr
CMD ["scripts/run_in_container.sh"]
```

Let's take a look at the instructions of the Api service Dockerfile.

1. The FROM command sets the base image for the rest of the instructions. In this case, we set the base image to openjdk:7.

2. The ENV instruction sets the environment variables for the container. In this case, we set our config file to config/api.test.properties, our heap size to 4G, our logs config file to config/log4j_local.xml.

3. Next, we set our working directory inside the container to /opt/api, using the WORKDIR instruction. This means that when you log in to your container, you will be inside the opt/api folder.

4. With the ADD instruction, we copy the folders to the container. First, we set the argument ARTIFACT_ PATH to target/api-0.1-SNAPSHOT-bin.tar. gz, using the ARG instruction, and next we copy this api-0.1-SNAPSHOT-bin.tar.gz file to the / opt/api folder inside the container. We also copy the target, scripts, and config folders on the host machine to the target, scripts, and config folders inside the container.

5. And, finally, we use the CMD instruction, which
    specifies the command for the image and does
    not execute it during build time. In this case,
    the command for the image is scripts/run_in_
    container.sh. This means that this script, run_in_
    container.sh, is used to get the Api service up and
    running.

Now that we have looked at the individual Dockerfiles of all three
services, let's take a look at some of the dependencies of those services.

First, let's take a closer look at the Client service and its dependencies.

```
<?xml version="1.0" encoding="UTF-8"?>
<project xmlns="http://maven.apache.org/POM/4.0.0"
xmlns:xsi="http://www.w3.org/2001/XMLSchema-instance"
xsi:schemaLocation="http://maven.apache.org/POM/4.0.0 http://
maven.apache.org/xsd/maven-4.0.0.xsd">
    <modelVersion>4.0.0</modelVersion>
    <groupId>funFeed</groupId>
    <artifactId>client</artifactId>
    <packaging>jar</packaging>
    <version>0.1-SNAPSHOT</version>
    <inceptionYear>2016</inceptionYear>
    <properties>
        <maven.compiler.source>1.8</maven.compiler.source>
        <maven.compiler.target>1.8</maven.compiler.target>
    </properties>
    <parent>
        <artifactId>client</artifactId>
        <groupId>client</groupId>
        <version>0.1-SNAPSHOT</version>
    </parent>
<dependencies>
```

```
<dependency>
    <groupId>com.twitter.common</groupId>
    <artifactId>args</artifactId>
    <version>0.2.41</version>
</dependency>
<dependency>
    <groupId>junit</groupId>
    <artifactId>junit</artifactId>
    <version>4.11</version>
    <scope>test</scope>
</dependency>
</dependencies>
```

If you look closely at the preceding code snippet, you will see that the Client service depends on JUnit version 4.11 and Twitter's com.twitter. common version 0.2.41, as noted below.

```
<dependency>
    <groupId>com.twitter.common</groupId>
    <artifactId>args</artifactId>
    <version>0.2.41</version>
</dependency>
<dependency>
    <groupId>junit</groupId>
    <artifactId>junit</artifactId>
    <version>4.11</version>
    <scope>test</scope>
</dependency>
```

Furthermore, the Client service also depends on certain plug-ins such as Puppycrawl.

```xml
<plugin>
                <groupId>org.apache.maven.plugins</groupId>
                <artifactId>maven-checkstyle-plugin</
                artifactId>
                <version>2.12.1</version>
                <executions>
                    <execution>
                        <id>verify-style</id>
                        <phase>process-classes</phase>
                        <goals>
                            <goal>check</goal>
                        </goals>
                    </execution>
                </executions>
                <dependencies>
                    <dependency>
                        <groupId>com.puppycrawl.tools</groupId>
                        <artifactId>checkstyle</artifactId>
                        <version>7.5.1</version>
                    </dependency>
                </dependencies>
</plugin>
        </plugins>
    </build>
</project>
```

As you can see in the preceding code snippet, the Client service depends upon the Puppycrawl tool version 7.5.1, in addition to the JUnit and Twitter dependencies.

Now, let's look at the requirements of the DB service.

```xml
<?xml version="1.0" encoding="UTF-8"?>
```

```xml
<project xmlns="http://maven.apache.org/POM/4.0.0"
xmlns:xsi="http://www.w3.org/2001/XMLSchema-instance"
xsi:schemaLocation="http://maven.apache.org/POM/4.0.0 http://
maven.apache.org/xsd/maven-4.0.0.xsd">
    <modelVersion>4.0.0</modelVersion>
    <groupId>funFeed</groupId>
    <artifactId>db</artifactId>
    <packaging>jar</packaging>
    <version>0.1-SNAPSHOT</version>
    <inceptionYear>2016</inceptionYear>
    <properties>
        <maven.compiler.source>1.8</maven.compiler.source>
        <maven.compiler.target>1.8</maven.compiler.target>
    </properties>
    <parent>
        <artifactId>db</artifactId>
        <groupId>db</groupId>
        <version>0.1-SNAPSHOT</version>
    </parent>
<dependencies>
    </dependencies>
```

As you can see from the preceding code, the DB service depends upon the JUnit and com.twitter.common library, as well, but on different versions of those libraries.

```xml
        <dependency>
            <groupId>com.twitter.common</groupId>
            <artifactId>args</artifactId>
            <version>0.2.39</version>
        </dependency>
        <dependency>
```

```xml
    <groupId>junit</groupId>
    <artifactId>junit</artifactId>
    <version>4.12</version>
    <scope>test</scope>
</dependency>
```

We already have versioning conflicts for JUnit and com.twitter.
common libraries, because both of these are used by both Client and
DB services, except that these services use different versions of these
libraries. If you were to run these services on a single machine on the same
application server, you would have to make these compatible with the
same version of JUnit and Twitter. Imagine doing this for 50 dependencies,
which could very well be the case for huge services. Then imagine adding a
new service that depends on the latest version of JUnit, in which case, you
would have to make all the previous services use the latest version of JUnit.
In addition, JUnit is a test-scoped dependency, so it isn't even included in
the final artifact. If a previous service was using a feature that is potentially
not supported in the latest version of JUnit, that would break your service,
and you would have to rewrite some of it to use the latest version of JUnit.
Nightmare! Isn't it?

Further, let's look at the Api service and its dependencies.

```xml
<plugin>
            <groupId>org.apache.maven.plugins</groupId>
            <artifactId>maven-checkstyle-plugin
            </artifactId>
            <version>2.10.1</version>
            <executions>
                <execution>
                    <id>verify-style</id>
                    <phase>process-classes</phase>
                    <goals>
```

```
                                <goal>check</goal>
                            </goals>
                        </execution>
                    </executions>
                    <dependencies>
                        <dependency>
                            <groupId>com.puppycrawl.tools</groupId>
                            <artifactId>checkstyle</artifactId>
                            <version>6.0.1</version>
                        </dependency>
                    </dependencies>
        </plugin>
            </plugins>
        </build>
</project>
```

Even though the Api service does not need JUnit or Twitter to execute,
it is dependent on the Apache Maven plug-ins and the Puppycrawl tool
plug-in, both of which are different versions than those of the Client
service, as you can see in the code snippet.

Even though there are conflicts in the dependencies of all these three
services, Docker can handle this gracefully, using one of its properties of
application isolation. That means that running these services individually
inside Docker containers will not cause these services to conflict with one
another. Instead, they can operate in their own isolated environment and
run simultaneously.

Alright, now that we have established why we are going to run these
services in Docker containers (to enable them running in their isolated
environments, to avoid conflict dependencies), let's look at how can we get
them all running together, so we can run the application end to end all at
once.

In the previous chapter, we looked at the Docker Compose tool and how and when to use it. In order to run our application from end to end, we will have to get all three services namely, Client, DB, and Api, up and running at the same time. We will use Docker Compose for this purpose.

```yaml
version: '3.8'
services:
  client:
    build:
      context: ./client
      dockerfile: Dockerfile-dev
    ports:
      - "5001:8887"
    command: "bash scripts/local_test_server.sh"
    container_name: client
    volumes:
      - "/home/{{USER}}/code/funFeed/client:/var/src/client"
      - "/var/serverset:/var/serverset"
      - "/var/config:/var/config"
    environment:
      - LOG4J_CONFIG_FILE=config/log4j.dev.properties
      - CONFIG_FILE=config/config_test.yaml
      - HEAP_SIZE=4G
      - NEW_SIZE=2G
      - CLASSPATH=/opt/client/cilent-0.1-SNAPSHOT

  db:
    build:
      context: ./db
      dockerfile: Dockerfile-dev
    ports:
      - "5004:9020"
    command: "bash scripts/run_in_container.sh"
```

```
container_name: db
volumes:
   - "/home/{{USER}}/code/funFeed/db:/var/src/db"
   - "/var/serverset:/var/serverset"
   - "/var/config:/var/config"
environment:
   - LOG4J_CONFIG_FILE=config/log4j_local.xml
   - CONFIG_FILE=config/db.test.properties
   - HEAP_SIZE=4G
   - NEW_SIZE=2G

api:
  build:
    context: ./api/server
    dockerfile: Dockerfile-dev
  ports:
    - "5005:8821"
  command: "bash scripts/run_dev_server.sh"
  container_name: api
  volumes:
     - "/home/{{USER}}/code/funFeed/api:/var/src/api"
     - "/var/serverset:/var/serverset"
     - "/var/config:/var/config"
  environment:
     - LOG4J_CONFIG_FILE=server/config/log4j.dev.properties
     - CONFIG_FILE=server/config/api.dev.properties
     - HEAP_SIZE=4G
     - NEW_SIZE=2G
     - CLASSPATH=/opt/api/api-server-0.1-SNAPSHOT
```

As you can see in preceding code snippet, the docker-compose file of
the FunFeed application contains the configuration of all three services
Client, DB, and Api.

Let's go through each instruction in this file.

1. services: The services key tells the docker engine all the services that constitute the application. In this case, the docker-compose.yaml file lives inside the FunFeed folder and contains three services, namely, Client, DB, and Api, as you can see in the preceding code snippet.

2. build: The build key specifies the context path and the path to the Dockerfile for each service.

3. ports: The ports key specifies which port on the container maps to which port on the host machine. In the preceding code snippet, under the Client service, you can see that port 8887 on the Docker container maps to port 5001 on the host machine.

4. command: This key specifies the command on image run. Under the Api service, you can see that the command for the Api service image run is bash scripts/run_dev_server.sh.

5. container_name: This key is the container name for the container in which that service runs in. For example, the container name for Client is client, that for DB is db, and that for Api is api.

6. volumes: This key specifies the volumes you want mapped from the host machine to the Docker container for each service.

7. environment: This specifies the environment variables for your Docker container.

Now that we've looked at our docker-compose file, let's go ahead and run this and see what it looks like.

The preceding docker-compose.yaml file is stored inside the FunFeed directory, where all three services that this application is composed of live in. In order to run your docker-compose file, you would go to your FunFeed directory and run docker-compose up.

```
kinnaryjangla@dev-abc:~/code/FunFeed$ docker-compose up

kinnaryjangla@dev-abc:~/code/FunFeed$ docker-compose up
Starting client  . . .
Starting client  . . . done
Starting db . . .
Starting db . . . done
Starting api . . .
Starting api . . . done
Attaching to client, db and api
api        | INFO: Admin HTTP interface started on port 8821.

db         | SLF4J: Class path container multiple SLF4J
             bindings.
db         | SLF4J: Found binding in [jar:file:/opt/db/db-
             0.1-SNAPSHOT/lib/logback-classic-1.jar!/org/
             slf4j/impl/StaticLoggerBinder.class]
db         | SLF4J: Found binding in [jar:file:/opt/db/db-
             0.1-SNAPSHOT/lib/slf4j-log4j12-1.6r!/org/slf4j/
             impl/StaticLoggerBinder.class]
db         | SLF4J: See http://www.slf4j.org/codes.
             html#multiple_bindings for an explanation.
db         | SLF4J: Actual binding is of type
             [ch.qos.logback.classic.util.
             ContextSelectorStaticBinder]
db         | Usage: java db config log4j_config
db         | INFO: Admin HTTP interface started
             on port 9020.
```

client		Jun 13, 2018 12:08:59 AM com.twitter.ostrich.admin.BackgroundProcess start
client		INFO: Starting PeriodicStatsLogger_delta_stats
client		Jun 13, 2018 12:08:59 AM com.twitter.ostrich.admin.BackgroundProcess start
client		INFO: Starting PeriodicStatsLogger_delta_stats
client		Jun 13, 2018 12:09:00 AM com.twitter.finagle.Init$$anonfun$1
client		INFO: Finagle version 6.25.0-p2 (rev=4963a777kag872691bdfsh92563vd72f4262)19
client		Jun 13, 2018 12:09:10 AM com.twitter.ostrich.admin.BackgroundProcess start
client		INFO: Starting PeriodicConfigLoader
client		Jun 13, 2018 12:09:10 AM com.twitter.common.zookeeper.Group$ActiveMembership join
client		INFO: Set group member ID to 00062c65282gdnkadhff82-87
client		Jun 13, 2018 12:09:10 AM com.twitter.ostrich.admin.BackgroundProcess start
client		INFO: Starting LatchedStatsListener
client		Jun 13, 2018 12:09:10 AM com.twitter.ostrich.admin.start
client		INFO: Admin HTTP interface started on port 9996.

As you can see, so far, we have Api and Client services running successfully. Next, let's verify whether Api, DB, and Client Docker containers are running.

Let's run `docker container ps` to view the containers running on the host machine as a result of `docker-compose`.

```
kinnaryjangla@dev-abc~/code/FunFeed$ docker container ps
CONTAINER ID             IMAGE       COMMAND                    CREATED
STATUS                   PORTS                        NAMES
d121c440051b             api     "bash scripts/loca..."   3 hours ago
Up 20 seconds        0.0.0.0-5001->8821/tcp         api
c7f77318fa0c             client   "bash scripts/loca..."  3 hours ago
Up 10 seconds        0.0.0.0-5001->8887/tcp         Client
ddfd9c2a35c4             db      "bash scripts/loca..."   3 hours ago.
Up 10 seconds        0.0.0.0-5001->9020/tcp          db
```

Now that we have all the Docker containers for all the services of our application up and running, as you can see in the preceding code snippet, let's see how we can look at the logs and how to look inside these Docker containers.

The `docker container logs` command shows logs from a running container.

```
docker logs [OPTIONS] CONTAINER
```

Additionally, you can log in to the Docker containers either by ID or by their name.

```
$ docker exec -I -t fa3cf9ad344c /bin/bash #by ID

$ docker exec -I -t api /bin/bash #by Name
```

```
$ root @fa3cf9ad344c:/opt/api:
```

Note, as you can see, the Dockerfile of the Api service sets the working directory to be /opt/api, which is why the container starts in that directory.

Now that we've looked at how to get inside the Docker containers, let's go ahead and query the entire FunFeed application.

The FunFeed application services talk to one another over a common network that could be defined in the docker-compose file. The Client service talks to the DB service, and the DB service talks to the Api service. This means that any incoming request from the Client service to the DB service will not go to the DB production service anymore. Instead, the request will be processed by the DB service running inside the Docker container named db. Similarly, any incoming request from the DB service to the Api service will go to the Api service running inside the Docker container named api.

Now that we're clear on how the request is going to get processed, it's time for the finale! Let's query our FunFeed application and see what we get back.

In order to query our application, make sure that you are inside the FunFeed ➤ client directory. Remember: client is our Client service, which will accept this request, authenticate the user, and send the user ID to the DB service, to get a list of interests for that user and then send it to the Api service, to get the list of images in the response.

Now, let's send this request to our Client service.

```
kinnaryjangla@dev-abc:~/code/FunFeed/client$ bash server/
scripts/client.sh -user_id=3456 -num_results=30
```

Let's look at what the preceding request means.

The server/local_test_serversh is the script that starts the server for the Client service, such that it gets ready to accept the incoming requests. The user_id is the parameter that is being passed to this script as an input.

"--" before user_id is just how the script recognizes what the input parameters are. num_results is a parameter that accepts the number of results.

Now let's look back at the preceding snippets. Observe that all three services are ready to accept incoming requests.

Now that we've made the request, let's go back and look at our web browser, because we have all our services hooked up to the correct ports (Figure 7-3).

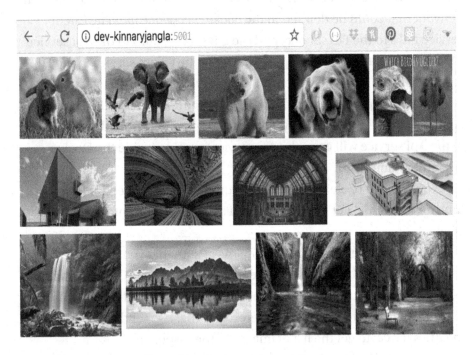

Figure 7-3. *FunFeed application results on the browser*

Now let's walk through what happened after we sent the request to the Client service.

1. The Client service took the request, parsed the user input (user_id and num_results) and sent this request to the DB service.

2. The DB service then authenticated the user ID.

3. The DB service then queried the MySQL database and looked up the user ID in the userIdToInterests SQL table, which had a mapping of the user ID to the Interests table.

4. The query resulted in a list of interests in the form of strings, such as animals, architecture, nature.

5. Once the DB service received this list, it then made a new request to the Api service, with this interest list as an input parameter.

6. The Api service queried the DbToImages table in the MySQL database and returned a list of images.

7. The Api service sorted the list of images it got back from the query.

8. The Api service then sent this list of images back to the DB service.

9. The DB service sent these images back to the Client service.

10. The Client service then rendered these images on the browser.

Note   There are many more optimizations that can be done in this application architecture, for example, storing images in a cloud-based storage or a CDN, improving latency by using HTTP accelerators or simple caching, breaking the DB service down into an authentication service and a service that is responsible for getting the interests list, etc. But all these optimizations are out of our scope. This application is simply to demonstrate how Docker can efficiently be used to render applications that have dependency conflicts with one another.

Furthermore, if you see in your terminal where the `client` Docker container is running, running the `docker container logs` command should show you everything that's happening inside each container. You should be able to see all the `post` and `get` requests being made and all data received. Remember: What you see in the logs is because of what your service and script logs on the output terminal. So, if you want more verbosity, make sure your script of your service logs the requests or the data that you would like to see in the logs. That also makes it easier to debug, if something is failing in any of these services.

Debugging

Now that we've looked at how an end-to-end application runs successfully on Docker, let's take a look at how you would debug if something failed here and what could be potential hurdles as you develop.

As you've seen so far, there are multiple things that must go right in order for the full application to run end to end. So, things could go wrong at multiple places. Let's look at a few and see how you'd debug them, if they occurred.

Dockerfile for an individual service has build errors.

- `Apt-get` is something that mostly all Dockerfiles might have. So, make sure you have that installed. It could potentially be out of date, and you might need an upgrade, so run `apt-get upgrade` to upgrade its version.

- Another reason could be that you're using `ADD` instead of `COPY`. In this case, first try to understand the difference between the two. `COPY` is a much easier command, because it simply copies the files from the host machine to the container.

ADD adds more complexity, because it includes more features, such as being able to add from a remote URL and auto-unpacking of compressed artifacts such as zip, tar, etc. If you don't need that simplicity, use COPY.

- If you're using :latest in your FROM command, the latest image might have been updated. To prevent this, you could use a certain version tag to be more specific about which exact build you are taking the base image from.

- You might have multiple FROM statements. Docker will always use the last one.

The docker-compose.yaml file has build errors.

- Make sure your Docker Engine is updated and that you have the right permissions to run the scripts and access the files.

- Make sure the docker-compose.yaml file is at the root of your project directory.

- Make sure your resources are not named with dots and dashes or any other illegal characters.

- Make sure you have access to the resources from the root directory.

- You might see an error from the Docker daemon, such as that following. Your solution here will be to run chmod +x scripts/run_in_container.sh, where you are making the script an executable file. Then rebuild the modules.

```
kinnaryjangla@dev-abc:~/code/FunFeed$ Error
response from doemon: oci runtime error: container_
linux.go:247: starting container process caused
"exec: \"script/run_in_container.sh\": permission
denied".
```

One of the services might exit with a certain error code

- When you run docker-compose up, one or more of
  the services might not start successfully.

- It might error with an exit code, as shown following.

- The error code 0 could really be anything.
  You could start first with running your script
  individually, using the bash command directly
  from your service directory, making sure the script
  runs and the service starts up successfully. If you're
  not able to get the script running successfully by
  itself, then there is either an issue with the way
  your service starts up or an error in the script itself.
  Narrowing down whether the script is an issue
  could be helpful.

```
db             |   SLF4J: Class path container
                   multiple SLF4J bindings.
db             |   SLF4J: Found binding in [jar:file:/
                   opt/db/db-0.1-SNAPSHOT/lib/logback-
                   classic-1.jar!/org/slf4j/impl/
                   StaticLoggerBinder.class]
db             |   SLF4J: Found binding in [jar:file:/
                   opt/db/db-0.1-SNAPSHOT/lib/slf4j-
                   log4j12-1.6r!/org/slf4j/impl/
                   StaticLoggerBinder.class]
```

```
db              | SLF4J: See http://www.slf4j.org/
                  codes.html#multiple_bindings for an
                  explanation.
db              | SLF4J: Actual binding is of type
                  [ch.qos.logback.classic.util.
                  ContextSelectorStaticBinder]
db              | Usage: java db config log4j_config
db exited with code 0
```

`service` could be crashing inside the Docker container.

- If everything else looks fine, but your service still exits with an error code, there is a possibility that your service could be crashing inside the Docker container it's running in.

- You can either look at the logs of the container using the `docker logs <container-name>` command, or you can log in inside the Docker container, then view whether the volumes are correctly mounted and the configurations are as per specifications, etc.

- Once inside the Docker container, you could also run the script to get the service up and running and make sure it has no permission issues.

Unused Docker containers

- Because you can spin up Docker containers so quickly, one thing to be aware of is that many unused Docker containers will simply keep consuming heaps of space on your machine.

- If you don't need these containers and images, feel free to remove them, so that they don't consume all that space.

- docker system prune, with or without options, can help with removing unused Docker containers, networks, or images that could be dangling, and even volumes, optionally. Some options that could be used are –all, which would remove all containers, and --volumes, which would prune volumes.

```
docker system prune [OPTIONS]
```

- Doing the preceding will ask you for a prompt, as shown following.

```
kinnaryjangla@dev-abc:~/code/FunFeed$ docker
system prune
WARNING! This will remove:
- all stopped containers
- all volumes not used by at least one container
- all networks not used by at least one container
- all dangling images
Are you sure you want to continue? [y/N]
```

Service discovery added overhead

- With the multi-tenancy territory comes an added overhead of discovering all these services. In our FunFeed example, I've left that out, as it is beyond our scope.

- In order to successfully launch an application running on a microservices architecture, you have to implement some kind of service discovery.

- In this day and age, with the rapid adoption of Docker, there are multiple solutions for this, such as ZooKeeper, Consul, etc.

- This overhead could potentially also cause issues while running docker-compose.

Last, docker-compose in theory is a very powerful and extremely straightforward tool to run multi-container applications. It's super convenient to get an application that is composed of multiple microservices up and running for development purposes and also in production environments.

Today, many companies, such as Pinterest, Lyft, Yelp, etc., run their services on Docker containers. In order for Docker containers to run at scale (to compute the resources needed to run containers), options such as Amazon Web Services (AWS) or any other public clouds come in very handy. AWS lets you deploy containers pretty quickly.

In addition, in order to get services running at scale in such large companies, automation of deployment of these services, also known as orchestration, requires different solutions. We'll look at that a little more in detail in the next and final chapter.

Summary

Phew, that was a lot! In this chapter, we looked at distributed environments and their advantages and challenges. You saw in depth that heterogeneity, concurrency, scalability, transparency, and failure handling are just a few of the issues related to distributed environments.

Later, we saw how an end-to-end application composed of microservices runs, using the Docker Compose tool. We walked through each service, its responsibility, individual Dockerfiles, the docker-compose file that runs the entire application, and, finally, we made a request to the entire end-to-end application, once all Docker containers were up and running. We saw the output of that request in a web browser. Last, we looked at some of the hurdles that you can encounter while running a full application on Docker.

In the next chapter, we'll look at how Docker works in production environments, how to scale Docker containers, and how all this ultimately helps us accelerate the development for software engineers.

CHAPTER 8

Advanced Docker Use Cases

In the previous chapter, you learned the advantages and challenges of distributed environments, such as heterogeneity, concurrency, scalability, transparency, and failure handling, to name just a few.

Later, I walked you through a sample end-to-end application called FunFeed, which, relying mainly on given user interests, renders a list of images on the users' feed related to those interests. We saw the different services that sit behind the application, got them running on their respective Docker containers, and then got all of these services up and running, using the Docker Compose tool. Finally, we made a request to the application and viewed the resulting output on the browser.

Toward the end of the chapter, I covered some hurdles you could face when setting up services in Docker and running the application end-to-end with the help of Docker Compose.

Now that you've seen most of the basic use cases of Docker, basic commands to get acquainted with Docker, how to get an end-to-end application running and debugged, it's time to view some advanced Docker use cases.

In this chapter, we'll look at how Docker operates in a production environment, orchestration using Docker, some advanced use cases, and, ultimately, some tips and tricks for Docker.

© Kinnary Jangla 2018
K. Jangla, *Accelerating Development Velocity Using Docker*,
https://doi.org/10.1007/978-1-4842-3936-0_8

In the last chapter, you gained some practical knowledge about running applications, based on microservices architecture, on Docker. That in itself is one of the basic use cases of Docker.

Let's look at what could have been done differently if that application were run in a production environment.

Docker in Production Environments

Now that we've got our application built and even running on Docker from our local machines, it might be time to ship it. Let's deploy it in our production environment, so that the world can start using it.

But wait, is our application really ready to be shipped? The answer is, not so fast!

There are many critical decisions to be made before we decide to ship our application. Let's look at some of them.

Managing Docker Images

We've seen in our previous chapters that Docker Hub is the public registry from which you both retrieve Docker images and publish to it, such that the images are made available to the world. However, when you want to make these images available to a smaller subset, such as the employees of a certain company, publishing them to the world won't really work.

You might want to set certain standards to write these images, for consistency and to avoid random local environment configurations, even though this process seemed quite straightforward in our development environments. Creating consistent standards for images will also help avoid dependencies on your development environment.

Given that we prefer to publish our images to a smaller subset and not the entire world, you'll have to set up a private Docker image registry. And, last, you'll want to make this private registry secure and available to your continuous deployment system.

136

Docker in Cloud

Now that you have your Docker image published in the right location, you'll have to deploy it to the Docker hosts. Today, most cloud providers, such as Amazon Web Services (AWS), Google Cloud, etc., provide support for deployment of Docker containers. These cloud providers charge for the resources, so the number can quickly turn up, and you might be in for a sticker shock.

Planning to host Docker strategically in the cloud might be your best option. Besides, the deployment process of Docker containers can vary from cloud provider to provider, making ramp-up curves difficult and time-consuming.

Security and Network

When working on a single development machine, you don't really have to worry about security or network access. There is no network intrusion, as such, because you're only dealing with a single host. Besides that, troubleshooting is pretty simple too, because again, it's a single machine you're dealing with.

Take that scenario and apply it to multiple hosts across a network in a production environment for scalability reasons. Your network settings will require a lot more thought. To begin with, only restricted people should have access to your Docker containers. Public traffic should not be able to touch certain containers. Tapping on the network, brute force login attempts, hacks, etc., must be supervised.

Security patches, whenever available, will have to be applied to all your Docker hosts. Using containers makes this much easier.

Load Balancing

Now that we're aware, that we'll require multiple hosts for scalability reasons, balancing this load across hosts is important. There are, however, multiple load balancers available today, such as ngapi.

Even though you could use one of these readily available load balancers, with Docker, creating and destroying containers could be common. This means that configuration settings will have to be updated every time a Docker container is created or destroyed.

Every time you deploy a new version of your application, your load balancer will have to take care not to drop traffic or rout it to the older version of your application.

Deployment

In a development environment, deploying and getting the services up and running is as simple as running `docker-compose up`. In a production environment, however, that might not be so simple. You will have to plan these in advance.

In a production environment, Docker Compose configurations will vary significantly from those in a development environment. In addition, as the traffic to your application increases, and as your application matures, you'll have multiple, continuous upgrades, hotfixes, and settings that must be consistent, resulting in abundant related issues to deal with on a continuous basis.

Service Discovery

Having an application with a growing number of microservices will require you to register these services. You'll have to find efficient ways of managing your service registries. There are multiple tools to do this, such as ZooKeeper.

Regardless of which tool you select to manage your service registry, one thing to be very sure of is to keep your service registrations in sync with your Docker container instances. Doing so will ensure that any new service registered is also recognizable by its Docker container instance.

Log Management

On a single development machine, we used `docker logs <container id>` to view the logs of an instance of a container. With multiple Docker hosts and services spread across these Docker hosts, troubleshooting becomes tedious. Distributed logging will have to be put in place to enable viewing of logs across containers, to troubleshoot issues.

Needless to say, logs will be long and numerous. You'll have to find a way to view and search these logs.

Monitoring Docker Containers

You'll have to watch the hosts and containers, to make sure they're healthy and not running out of space. You'll have to know the health of the entire system and each individual service as well.

You'll need to have certain monitoring strategies in place for this. Tools such as Grafana can help you achieve this.

Managing Databases

In development environments, databases can be hosted in a single container, without having to worry about input/output (I/O) performance. This changes in a production environment. I/O performance becomes essential, especially if you care to provide a good consumer experience. Your database will have to scale and be highly available, in order to maintain good I/O performance.

These are only some of the challenges that you might encounter when you make the decision to take your application to production. Docker provides some amazing capabilities, but in spite of that, there are certain other tools required to make scalability more efficient, because Docker is not a full-blown architecture service. It's a tool and that's all.

Orchestration Using Docker

What is container orchestration, after all? Put simply, a container orchestration is the process of deploying multi-container applications on multiple machines. Or, even more essentially, it's the process of transitioning individual containers on a single host to multi-container applications on multiple machines.

Needless to say, in order to achieve this, one would require a distributed platform that can stay online through the entire lifetime of an application, surviving hardware and software failures and upgrades.

In order to enable orchestration, Docker came up with a solution known as "Docker in swarm mode."

Basically, it consists of a group of Docker Engines on which applications can be deployed using the Docker API. API objects such as Service and Node can be used to do this.

There are multiple tools that can be used for orchestration, for example, Kubernetes. One way to orchestrate Docker is with Docker! Docker orchestration is built in as part of the core Docker Engine, and it relies on some fundamental principles, such as simplicity, reliability, security, and backward compatibility.

Modern distributed applications that serve heavy traffic are mostly all going to run on multiple hosts and multiple machines and, therefore, will require orchestration as a critical element. More often than not, a new tool comes on the market, and developers must ramp up on it quickly. Before you know it, some other tool supersedes it, and it's time to ramp up on that.

Simplicity of tools makes it easier for developers to start using them more quickly. At the same time, making these tools more powerful allows developers to use them for longer periods of time, thus providing more flexibility. Docker in swarm mode takes advantage of this fundamental principle. And it's built with simplicity in mind, yet it's one of the most powerful tools. It focuses on resilience in addition to simplicity. Computers fail all the time, and systems should expect that and be able to adapt to potential failures effortlessly.

Needless to say, applications built on distributed systems must be highly secure. Security should be an assumed principle. Continuous upgrades of certificates, privacy updates, network tapping, etc., are effortlessly incorporated in the swarm mode.

Docker has had multiple versions and millions of users using these different versions. For this reason, maintaining backwards compatibility is essential for Docker, and that's exactly what Docker in swarm mode provides.

Advanced Use Cases

Let's look where else Docker containers have left their mark and where they're currently being used for advanced uses.

- *Land Information System (LIS)*: LIS is owned by NASA and has been extremely difficult to install, owing to its complexity and its dependencies on other complex libraries. With Docker, scaling LIS has been relatively simpler and, hence, has made it available to a larger group of users. Docker has also made LIS installation simpler. So, in this case, NASA uses Docker to simplify its installation process and improve its scalability rather than helping to achieve continuous delivery.

- *Local area network (LAN) caches*: An interesting example of an obscure use case is using Docker for setting up a LAN cache. This allows you not to have to deal with the grungy work that comes with setting up a LAN party. Even though this might be a typical Docker use case, it's definitely one that's very interesting.

- *Government software*: Docker has been quietly helped by federal government software, which is a universe all its own. Docker has been proven helpful in achieving the security and privacy needed in complex government software.

- *Bioinformatics*: Many bioinformatics programs have been using Docker to build their own Docker registries for bioinformatics tools and software. BioShaDock is an exclusive bioinformatics repository for bioinformatics programs. This differentiates it from a public Docker registry.

- *Internet of Things (IoT)*: Not surprisingly, Docker has entered the IoT realm as well. Resin.io leverages Docker for its deployment of IoT devices.

Tips and Tricks

Now that we've looked at some obscure but interesting use cases of Docker, let's quickly take a look at some tips and tricks that can come in handy when debugging your Docker application.

- *HTTP proxy*: A typical Dockerfile starts with a FROM, with which you pull a public image from the Docker registry. This means it will have to be pulled from the Internet. Note the following code snippet:

```
FROM tifayuki/java:8
MAINTAINER . . .
RUN apt-get update \
wget download.java.net/glassfish/4.0/release/glassfish-
4.0.zip \
. . .
```

You might run into an issue if you're behind a proxy.
In this case, you can set up your proxy using the ENV
command in your Dockerfile. So, your Dockerfile
will look like the following snippet:

```
FROM tifayuki/java:8
MAINTAINER . . .
ENV http_proxy http://server:port
ENV https_proxy http://server:port
#. . . some other online commands
```

- *Listing all existing containers*: You can use `docker container ps -a` to list all your containers. This will list containers that have stopped running as well.

- *Stopping all running containers*: Using `docker container stop $(docker container ps -a -q)` will stop all running containers.

- *Deleting all existing containers*: `docker container rm $(docker container ps -a -q)` will delete all your existing containers. To remove containers that are still running, you can use the −f flag. So, your command would look like Docker container rm −f.

- *Deleting all existing images*: `docker image rm $(docker image ls -aq)` will let you delete all your existing images.

143

- *Using the* CMD *command in Dockerfile*: CMD and RUN are two commands that can become confusing when trying to determine what to run when. RUN runs the command, then commits the result at the time of build. The CMD command mainly provides defaults for a running container. It should be used inside a Dockerfile only once, and it runs the software in your image at runtime.

Summary

In this chapter, I reviewed the decisions that you'll have to make, in order to take your Docker application to production. You saw how network access and security, deployment of multiple Docker containers and multiple Docker hosts, etc., can be quite challenging.

You then saw how Docker has a swarm mode to help with orchestration, which is managing complex multi-container applications on multiple machines. You also learned some tips and tricks that can be very useful when building applications with Docker.

This concludes this book. All the knowledge you've gained, if put into practice, can tremendously increase the velocity of your software engineering.

Index

A
Amazon Web Services
       (AWS), 133, 137

B
Bioinformatics, 142

C
Command-line interface
       (CLI), 30
Container-based virtualization, 7
Container orchestration
    distributed systems, 141
    Docker API, 140
Containers
    advantages, 6–7
    benefits, 3
    definition, 2
    disadvantages, 7–8
    host computer, 5
    running applications,
           virtual machine, 6
    vs. virtual machines, 3–5
Cost-effective solution, 7

D
Database schema, 21
Debugging, 103
    docker-compose.yaml file, 129
    Docker container, 131
    error code, 130
    FunFeed (*see* FunFeed
           application)
    individual service, 128
    service discovery, 132
Distributed application bundle
       (DAB), 87
Distributed system
    advantages
        data sharing, 101
        scaling methods, 100
    challenges
        complexity, 102
        concurrency, 102
        debugging, 103
        failure handling, 103
        heterogeneity, 101
        scalability, 102
Docker
    advantages, 13
    architecture

© Kinnary Jangla 2018
K. Jangla, *Accelerating Development Velocity Using Docker*,
https://doi.org/10.1007/978-1-4842-3936-0